SOC

EDUCATION AND MORAL WISDOM

EDUCATION AND MORAL WISDOM

BY GEORGE N. SHUSTER
PRESIDENT, HUNTER COLLEGE

FOREWORD BY ORDWAY TEAD

HARPER & BROTHERS, NEW YORK

EDUCATION AND MORAL WISDOM

FOREWORD
BY ORDWAY TEAD
CHAIRMAN, BOARD OF HIGHER EDUCATION OF
NEW YORK CITY (1938–1953)

GEORGE NAUMAN SHUSTER BECAME PRESIDENT OF HUNTER COLLEGE in 1939. In addition to earlier university teaching posts in his field of English he had been conspicuously successful as editor of the liberal Catholic organ *The Commonweal.*

Here was a singular combination of churchly upbringing and religious association with subsequent immersion in the duties of a public and therefore secular institution of higher learning.

The polarity of a deeply devout Church past and the leadership of a public college for young women and now for young men also helps to supply a key to the *leitmotif* of his career and his brilliant achievement in conducting and interpreting the role of the American college as these chapters succeed in doing.

The essays comprising this volume were largely occasional pieces. But each had the basic purpose of affirming the spiritual roots and moral overtones of all American education with its historic democratic convictions and purposes.

It is good that in a period when secularity and logical positivism, if not a callow scientism, have been rampant in the colleges, Dr. Shuster has been so notably able to sound always the note of moral wisdom.

A sensitive, devout, learned, and widely ranging personality—his utterances reflect the man in at once an accurate and a noble manner.

Dr. Shuster's interpretations of education affirm with convic-

v

tion, power, and persuasiveness the inward elevation of the American college at its best.

He is an exponent in a fluid and distinctive prose of all that is finest in the American college aspiration, public and private. His articulateness is as cogent as his vision.

To mark his retirement after twenty years in a congenial post of leadership it is thus most appropriate to signalize the rounding out of a mission to young people by making accessible to a widening audience his insights as to why and how it is that higher education is not alone an intellectual experience but at its best adds to this vital function the call to moral duty and spiritual insight which marks this volume.

It is not surprising, therefore, that all of those who have been the beneficiaries of his leadership should join in a common effort to commemorate a significant period in the life of the college. The students of Hunter College and its constituent schools, their faculties and staffs, the members of the Board of Higher Education, the college's alumni and other organizations which have grown and flourished during the past decades have, through their representatives, planned a tribute to George Shuster which takes a triple form.

A Faculty Fellowship Fund bearing George Shuster's name has been established to aid the scholars of the college to continue and to amplify their research. This will commemorate and give practical force to President Shuster's deep conviction that the vitality of the college can be preserved and enhanced only if its faculty continue vigorously in the academic tradition of scholarship and research.

A portrait of Dr. Shuster is to be painted by a distinguished American artist. It will be hung as a treasured possession of the college, to preserve for those who will form the Hunter College of the future the image of his urbane and charming person.

Lastly, there is this book which well reflects the quality of George Shuster's mind.

The president has written a number of books which have commanded the attention and respect of a wide circle of readers.

His thoughtful reviews of the books of others have been many and influential. But to those of us who know him best, it is in his briefer articles, and above all in his addresses to academic audiences, that he shows most clearly the indomitable originality of his mind. Though the individual pieces are spaced irregularly through some fifteen of the twenty years which we commemorate, and though no one of them was written with any thought of its relationship to the others, there runs through all of them the golden thread of a cogent educational credo. Learning and wisdom without moral purpose, he has always held, are unworthy of their lofty names.

It is a matter of no little gratification to record, finally, my personal satisfaction in having played a small part as a college trustee and now as publisher of this testimony to educational insight. It comes as a welcome contribution to the wider audience today concerned to raise the sights of excellence and of moral worth in the conduct of our colleges.

CONTENTS

EDUCATION AND
MORAL WISDOM

THE ADMINISTRATION
OF A
MUNICIPAL COLLEGE*

I HAVE SOMETIMES PERMITTED MYSELF TO BELIEVE THAT COLLEAGUES in the fraternity of college presidents might profitably read two great treatises on education—Don Quixote and the dramas of Euripides—which are not alluded to as frequently as seems desirable. In the one there is to be found a terse and searching discussion of what happens to the public mind when values are ignored and integrity is dissipated; and in the other a man of notable wisdom and experience weighs the limitations of the intelligence and the perils that attend what are known as intuitions or urges. But the mere use of the term, "great book," makes many a lip quiver. While it is true that Matthew Arnold counseled seeking out "the best that has been known and thought in the world," our contemporaries often appear to feel that to call anything "best" is to commit an act of metaphysical obscurantism. To legislate that two times two are four would, one surmises, be deemed undemocratic effrontery; and if so unpardonable an offense were perpetrated, the matter would no doubt eventually be referred to the Supreme Court, which body might well opine that two and two are seven, with Mr. Justice Reed demurring, and Mr. Justice Frankfurter delivering a classic and quite competently documented defense of the traditional view.

The mixture of opinions now served up is, in short, so very

* Reprinted from *Goals for American Education: Ninth Symposium*, edited by Lyman Bryson and others (New York: Harper and Brothers, 1950), pp. 373–384.

like a traffic jam that it has become almost impossible for any number of people to proceed in any direction together. The other day I was invited to comment on an article, accepted for publication by one of the more popular magazines, which called for the condoning of murder when the victims could not be proved to have been socially useful beings. The author, it appeared, believed that a great many people would serve humanity most effectively by assenting in advance to their somewhat untidy demises. I remonstrated rather feebly that there existed no evidence to prove that the writer of the piece was not hoist by his own petard, and suggested that it was quite unfair to propose so beguiling a temptation as this sort of homicide to one so weak as I am. The incident is related here because it strengthened an impulse to live anew with Euripides in my pocket and Don Quixote on my desk. The educational ideal which is here taken for granted is, as a result, fairly simple and uncomplicated.

I hold it to be the first business of a college to be a friendly, literate, and sometimes amusing place, in which a relatively few things are taken very seriously, indeed. They do not include the integration of the curriculum, or even the elimination of vocational courses in favor of a vigorous emphasis on abstract thought. I shall enumerate them. First, a person who is not deeply interested in teaching and more than willing to work hard at it ought not to take money for being employed by a college, however important his research may be. Second, the college, if it is to be any good, must provide the instructor with some little place on the campus which he can call his own, and in which he can confer with students—in short it must equip Mark Hopkins with a log. Third, some provision must be made for listening to what the students themselves think of the proceedings. And fourth, the young people who come should be expected to work as hard as other young people do who are not in college. An institution which lives by these principles will, I think, win the allegiance of its students, and its alumni will see to it that it has support. I do not consider it my professional obligation to save souls, or even to make an atomic age say to itself each morning that it is the atomic age.

As I see it, my business as an administrator is to try to create a college such as I have described. The situation prevailing at a municipal college is of course in some respects different, and an attempt will be made in what follows to outline the problems and to set forth some of the efforts being made to solve them. It is abundantly clear, of course, that effort is not success. It is often just an experiment, or perhaps an act of trusting to luck in the absence of recipes which can be guaranteed to produce results.

A municipal college may be defined as one financed out of the city treasury, administered by a Board of Higher Education, and subject to the provisions of the education law of the state. This means that the administrator must work inside a sort of triple enclosure, the presence of which he is often made aware of by a bump to his bones. Cities are no doubt much alike, but I can speak at first hand only of New York. This has been very generous to higher education, though its budgetary procedures are by no means as elastic as are those of many states. That is at once an advantage and a handicap. One can be reasonably sure of avoiding drastic curtailments, but one must also realize early that one's native eloquence, however remarkable, will not loosen the purse strings to any memorable extent. In my time I have found the city administration notably honest and unbiased. Indicating that this is true has done no harm. Woe betide the man who is in debt for political favors! But let us extend our regrets also to him who is not generously aware of the virtues of those who are in political life.

A Board of Higher Education—or a similar board under whatever name—differs from a board of trustees serving a private college in that its members are seldom selected from among the graduates of the institution. They are appointed to represent important component groups of the population, and for this reason will normally be public-spirited citizens who are sincerely interested in education. They are therefore without any special sentimental attachment to a given college, but they are likely to manifest a deep concern for fair play, honesty of administration, and faculty welfare, while strongly opposing any kind of intolerance or quackery. Sometimes a member of the board may ride his own hobbies, or put all his eggs into one basket. But on the whole I believe that the great majority of municipal college presidents will say that their cities have appointed year after year ladies and gentlemen who continue to be regarded affectionately as ladies and gentlemen; who support the presidents of their choosing loyally and intelligently; and whose awareness of community feeling has been proved a dependable barometer. It costs heavily in time and money to be a member of a board, and if anything goes wrong one is in the doghouse. Nevertheless I cherish the feeling that nearly all board members I have known considered the sacrifice worthwhile. The administrator must learn to work with such men and women and to respect their opinions even when they diverge sharply from his own. In view of the fact that the powers of publicly appointed boards are likely to be very broad, and that in the final analysis responsibility is coupled with power, it seems to me quite surprising that so few major decisions prove to be utterly wrong.

State education laws differ, and so I shall use that of New York as an illustration. It is a many-faceted and important document. It confers tenure and salary upon teachers, so that on the one hand these teachers are likely to be frozen into their posts very early, while on the other hand movements to improve the economic status of the faculty proceed quite independently of the administration of the college and are supported with such pressure as the staff itself can muster. The law also limits freedom of instruction, particularly in the sense that anything smacking of religious exhortation is taboo. Personally I consider this ban an anachronism. It is of course undesirable that students belonging to different churches or creeds be subjected unilaterally to teaching which incorporates the dogmas of any one church or creed. But just why one should be so squeamish about the presentation of religious views to students who desire to see such views expounded remains a mystery. And of course the outcome is that opinions detrimental to any religious point of view must likewise be exorcised.

So much for the framework. Perhaps the sorest trial which a college administrator thus constrained is likely to encounter at the outset is the realization that the alma mater he fosters is looked upon as a poor relation. So sacred to the American are ivy and private property that an institution which charges very little, if anything at all, which admits children regardless of the status of their ancestors, and which probably does not list among its alumni many Presidents of the United States, is often considered the habitat of unfortunate beings who, but for the absent-mindedness of the taxpayer, would be scouring pans for the rest of their lives. Therefore the administrator husbands every ounce of prestige as carefully as Mr. Lilienthal does atomic energy. His big task is to convince his own students and faculty that they can look the world in the face with confidence. Unless he is perennially careful the morale of his institution will bog down like a Buick on a Ukrainian dirt road. He must, with a kind of virtuous unscrupulousness, take advantage of every bit of glitter he can amass; and yet he must at the same time remain intellectually honest and, indeed, just the least bit cynical.

He profits from the fact that his student material is the best in the world. The great majority of the youngsters who come to his college have a price tag on their chests. It would be far more advantageous economically for their families if after leaving high school they got some sort of a job—if they addressed envelopes or wrapped parcels in a department store. But a deep respect and hunger for learning persists, together with the hope that eventually the scion of hard-working parents may strut the stage in a better role. Students, therefore, have all the faults of American youth save one. They seldom feel that Dad will bail them out even if their four years at college are what my contemporaries defined as a complete "flop." They may write atrocious English. They may never have heard of Emily Post. But they are not vagabonds on their way to and from the Social Register. They need to be cajoled a little, and to be prodded more than a little.

They are the salt of the earth which has to find out what salt is. And we fail miserably whenever they do not find out.

You must remember that such students will not often be taught by the most glamorous of American teachers. Sometimes indeed —and I regret to say this—they are addressed by instructors who entertain a profound contempt for their charges, and compensate for their nostalgic evocations of Oxford by looking about them with aversion. But it is pleasant to note that while a municipal college may not number among its employees many of the most highly touted, it does assemble some of the most devoted of professors. These are men and women who have plumbed at first hand the meaning of scholarship but who remain nonetheless the patient guides and friends of youth; who have trained their hearts to draw no line of demarcation between student and student for any extraneous reason; and who, if they themselves have risen from among the less widely acclaimed sections of the population have, while surrendering no cherished principle of religious belief or national heritage, put on a garment one can only refer to as charity because it is more luminous than humanism, is indeed the product of faith in the meaningfulness of the origin and destiny of man.

To build a community of the best of such students and their teachers, against the background of numerous and diverse urban homes (for the municipal college student does not live on the campus) is no doubt the basic, continuing problem. There are so many young people that one cannot hope to know any great number of them. But one can recall that nothing is so sacred to college students as are traditions, and proceed to create things that will be remembered—say, a Christmas assembly and luncheon, with community singing; a place in which to browse among books, or to argue incessantly; a bench on which sitting is forbidden, and therefore especially attractive. One can make an effort to help young people through a program of guidance that makes sense because it deals on a personal basis with each individual girl or boy.

Above all one must put no credence in either of two favorite myths. One must not believe that merely taking a program in the liberal arts will equip a youngster who has no arrows in her bow for hitting the bull's-eye which is a livelihood. I could illustrate in a thousand ways the quite pathetic helplessness of graduates who despite the reading they have done in Thucydides and Homer have not the foggiest notion about what action to take in order to fit in somewhere. An aspect of the liberal arts myth which invites special criticism is that which has to do with what one may term inculcated high-mindedness. This is something quite different from honesty, loyalty, humility, or any other of the traditional virtues. It is a state of being so chock-full of good advice to the world that one has literally moved out of the world. One could be a United States Senator, no doubt, or possibly even a Vice President. But that one should be destined to toil as a clerk in the office of the Peterkin Thermos Bottle Company, or to change diapers, or to market cigars, is first of all incredible and secondly utterly disillusioning. I may add that we who are along in years too often forget that the average young person has to be pushed first out of home and then out of college. At home, Mother is a factotum, supplying everything from cereal to television. And at college the dean is currently a sort of expanded incubator, which can hatch every problematical egg. But whereas the fledgling bird need only learn how to fly and how to grub for a worm, the young being must make a difficult social and psychological adjustment to living—so difficult, indeed, that the market for books which purport to explain how it is to be done is always a staggeringly profitable one.

The municipal college cannot afford to be unrealistic about such matters. I have unshamefacedly urged all language and literature majors to take courses in typewriting and stenography, and I have just as persistently cajoled feminine students into finding out what a baby looks like, what has to be done to help it grow up, and what a strange sort of creature its father is likely to be. Yes, I am persuaded that the issues here alluded to are so important that until they have been dealt with any further extension of college facilities might well be relatively catastrophic.

I concede that perhaps society ought to reimburse everyone who can sing an aria from *Martha;* but if the singers have to take up a collection from amongst themselves, because the performers outnumber the audience, something has gone wrong, and it is not the capitalist system. I believe in the values of education as ardently as does anyone else. But it seems to me inconceivable that a college exists in order to help young people fail in everything else than their classes.

Now for the second myth. Can we really teach students either professions or vocations? The anwer is, of course, no. A man qualifies for such a calling as medicine or law by taking advantage of what a school can offer him, of what he finds out afterward, and of what he has in himself. A good physician is a man of knowledge, character, insight, and magnanimity. And the really bad doctor is not the quack who "cures" arthritis with herb tea, but the impostor who sells patients his wholly worthless degree. Accordingly there is little need to point out that what an undergraduate college can do to help train students to be writers or concert pianists, advertising salesmen or teachers, is relatively insignificant. But it is equally apparent that it can do something. One can, for example, foster a bent toward journalism by providing some sort of work experience that resembles journalistic activity. Harm is done only when more is attempted than can be essayed realistically—when, for instance, the teaching of educational psychology in segments as numerous as are the products of Heinz is looked upon as a satisfactory preparation for classroom instruction.

In short I do not believe in the "pure" college, the sole business of which is to feed its infants an extract of world culture. The value of the Hutchins "great books" idea seems to me to lie not in the choice of the books (though it is a pretty good one) but rather in the proposed method of studying them. This method is a revamping of what the French call *explication de texte,* which in turn is part of the age-old teaching of rhetoric, designed to train orators, lawyers, statesmen, and teachers. One has only to note that Mr. Winston Churchill's words have played so significant a part in modern history because like Cicero's they were hammered on the anvil of a great intellectual and art tradition, in order to see that by bringing to life again, though perhaps with a larger number of cabalistic signs than was wholly necessary, the teaching of rhetoric, in the true sense, Mr. Hutchins has rendered a very important service to our democracy. This democracy must assume that each citizen is in some modest way a statesman. It is not "culture" that Mr. Hutchins is trying to sell (whether he knows it or not) but the art of becoming a cultivated and communicative man.

But I do not see why the cult of the *disputatio* and the *colloquium* should be hermetically sealed off from contact with vocational or work experiences such as I have described. In my lifetime, which included formative years spent in a gymnasium of the Swiss type, I think I have learned that some strenuous thinking about what one is going to do as well as about what one is going to be, is a vital part of growing up. And so our own college pattern of instruction includes always some room for what, for lack of a better term, I have called "vocational inlays," and which may be described as modest essays in the art of preparing for life. At any rate, our record seems to indicate that such inlays give the student confidence and a sense of direction. Our difficulty is not one of finding that vocational considerations occupy too much of our time. It is rather that we cannot soon enough give our students some insight into the ultimate unifying purpose of their collegiate life.

Here, of course, we, too, are brought face to face with the enigma which everybody is discussing and with which, alas, a college administrator can do nothing as an administrator but only as a sort of philosopher or even poet—which even if he were able he could seldom find time to be. The root of the problem is obviously this: the college, like the university, exists to husband, distribute, and even to increase knowledge; but the deepest insight into the meaning and the drift of life comes not from knowledge but from belief. By belief I do not mean credulity but a willing personal venture, exacting and even at times heartrending, amidst the eternal landmarks of holiness, awe, universally valid law, tragedy, and comedy. Just as the college cannot produce genius or great poetry, so also is it unable to inculcate sanctity or wisdom. Knowledge will remain forever the centrifugal activity of the mind face to face with reality. It is the quest for the parts of which the whole is compounded; and each part is in turn so infinitely complex that in its microcosm one rediscovers the endless depth that the world everywhere manifests.

Therefore when I personally talk of these things I try to say that the experience of knowing, of accumulating knowledge, is valuable because of the dexterity, accuracy, and perspective which it can bring to one's performance of the quite relative tasks one is to assume in an always necessarily relative human world. Knowledge, in other words, is functional. It will help a doctor to diagnose and properly deal with pneumonia, and it will assist the psychologist in warding off some potentially dangerous psychosis. The proper teaching of rhetoric would revitalize what are called the humanities. But one cannot alter the fact that man's existence, like the existence of the cosmos, is a profound mystery, the confrontation of which by each human being is his personal religious experience. Perhaps art and literature and philosophy can bring one to this point. Beyond that each single soul is on its own. I believe it would be well to express openly and humbly such a sense of the limitations of education. Knowledge cannot be integrated. It may within limits be more rationally organized, and possibly it may also be quite tentatively synthesized into what is called "general knowledge." But should we really succeed even if we added the encyclopedia to the hundred best books? Integration in the ultimate, final sense is something quite different. It is silence.

So then I go back to where we were before. A good college is a place where a young generation associates with older generations in order to learn how to be useful and cultivated participants in the business of life. This living together should be as good-spirited, stimulating, industrious, and courteous as possible, because in the end a civilization is worth saving only if it is these

things. One has the right to go home smiling at the foibles of
one's colleagues and oneself. But one is forever stigmatized by
pettiness and pride. The good teacher, in a word, is a good friend.
He can utter the truth that hurts, but only because he realizes
also that it can heal.

If I may at the end formulate a few opinions about some of the
special problems of the municipal college, I shall single out two
from among so many that the mere enumeration of them would
be confusing. First, this college is an integral part of the community it serves. Like the public school, it is more than a school
—is, in fact, a sort of "center" to which the neighborhood and it
may be the city as a whole look for a variety of services. Second,
a municipal institution, being nonresidential, cannot provide opportunity for the experience of living in common under direction
which is among the noblest duties performed by a good campus
college, and which is rooted in the age-old monastic practice of
idealistic intellectuals, of whatever creed or persuasion. This experience is one for which our age, formed by individualism,
ardently yearns, as witness on the one level such movements as
the French Resistance and even, when they are young and fer-
vent, Communist cells, or, on the other hand, such evocations of
a pattern of living as that of Hermann Hesse in *Das Glasperlen-
spiel*, which won for its author the Nobel Prize.

Viewed as a community center, the municipal college offers a
broad program of what, for lack of a better term, is called "adult
education." There are formal cultural and vocational courses;
supervised activities which are properly recreational in character;
and such more ambitious enterprises as the Hunter College Concert Series. And, in addition, room and facilities are made available to a great variety of educational and cultural groups,
sometimes famous as is the Boston Symphony Orchestra and
sometimes young and experimental. The fostering of such associations and the selection of those which most merit what is
always looked upon as approval by the college is an important
administrative function. I think that these various kinds of community education are bound to prove more and more significant.

There is still a good deal of feeling around in the dark here, and more than a little charlatanism. But I am convinced that the answer to America's educational problem does not lie in the multiplication of colleges at which still other tens of thousands will spend four years. It is to be found rather in a decision so to reorganize secondary education that young people will be channeled into the working and culturally advancing community in accordance with their aptitudes and abilities, and then to create a virile and creative "adult education" movement to which a portion of leisure time can be devoted.

This is manifestly a complex and difficult topic, which cannot be elaborated here. It is apparent, however, that the college administrator cannot run away from it—and that he cannot persist in the leisurely belief that four years of life on the campus will be significant at all unless they are rich in meaning for the whole lives of the individuals affected. Let us also note that while it is most certainly true that no qualified young person should be denied the benefits of higher education because of inability to pay for those benefits, it is also true that Ph.D. degrees cost more than they ever have before and that, in purely economic terms they are worth less than they have ever been worth. But the participation of the whole community in the making of its common culture is above all price.

Viewed as a "city pavement" institution, the municipal college assuredly needs supplementing with some place in the country, supported in part by the students themselves, at which they can participate for limited periods of time in a community building experience. Out of such experience altruism will grow, and altruism is the indispensable concomitant of leadership. I hope that my own college will in the not too far distant future have such facilities available, and I am sure that the use we can make of them could be rewarding beyond all claims that I could now make. There would then be ready for realization a pattern of education in which life in the home environment would conjoin with initiation into the academic community, in order to humanize the fruits of study.

I have said these are problems among many. To state them even briefly is to make evident once more that the job of a college administrator is one which no human being in his right mind would willingly assume. One takes on such assignments when one is momentarily drunk with a vision of what might be accomplished if one were somebody else and the world a more malleable affair than it unfortunately is, and muses then during subsequent hours of relative sobriety upon one's limitations, errors, and inability to surmount circumstances. One sees clearly then that if one were Augustine, one would still have a tiff with one's colleague, Jerome, and that if one were Plato, the *Republic* would get itself on paper well enough but not off it again. But one is not Augustine or Plato but only a rather dowdy duffer of a little more than middle age, wondering where the next eruption is likely to take place. And perhaps that is as it should be. One must have a stout heart, a tough skin, a sense of humor, and somewhere in the background like an icon in a crypt a core of unflinching and indestructible honor. One can then safely permit oneself to marvel daily at the glory and the beauty of youth, without minding too much the portent of the dire fate which will some day be meted out to it also—the fate of starting all over again for its successors the process to which it itself is subjected.

THE
AMERICAN OCCUPATION
AND
GERMAN EDUCATION*

EDUCATION, IF WE VIEW IT ARIGHT, IS A CEASELESS KNOCKING AT
the door. Young people appear. They are not very different from
the countless other young people who in past ages have struggled
to grow up. Everything that happens round about them pounds
on the drums of their sensibilities with never to be forgotten
resonance in the fullest meaning of the term. The language their
parents speak sets up a chain of echoes from which they may
struggle to escape, while in school and out of it, but which in the
long run will have wound itself about their limbs. The longer I
live the more convinced I become that the central problem of
the educator is this: Can the chain be transformed into the ma-
terials of a ladder up which the individual may climb to a long-
range perception of himself and of the reality which surrounds
him? To throw away the past is not the intent of either God or
nature. For the past is the only ground on which a human being
can stand. He cannot place his feet upon the future because he
has no way of telling where the future may be. But if he says
that his business is not to reach the unknown that is to be, the
spirit of adventure cannot in any way have enlightened him.

It is against the background of some such dynamic philosophy
of education that one must place the history of efforts to reform

* Reprinted from *Proceedings of the American Philosophical Society* 97
(1953), pp. 159–162.

German academic life. For the idea to which the victors origi-nally subscribed was that the legacy of domestic and scholastic training in Germany was wholly evil, since it had produced nazism. Accordingly, the German past was deemed worthy of destruction. There were several different senses in which the process of demolition was understood. The Russians came out for thoroughly secularized schools which would offer as little resistance as possible to the imbibing of their social and scientific panaceas. The British went in largely for letting the youth of a dismantled Germany do pretty much what they had always done, subject to rather casual purges of Nazi teachers and ma-terials. The French viewed the situation as made to order for the advertisement of their own cultural achievements, which are considerable, and so brought to the Germans a great variety of discourses, exhibitions, and concerts which the educated public undoubtedly enjoyed very much. Americans dissented from all these methods. We thought the important thing was to drive the germs of nazism out of the German system with a variety of wonder drugs, the more important of which had long since purged the United States of all uncleanness.

On the one hand, we were still of the opinion that Russia was a democracy, even if a somewhat crotchety one, and so took a keen interest in demonstrating that we were democratic, too. We, therefore, directed an attack on what was defined as a "class-conscious" educational system. This assault was carried out with such weapons as free textbooks for all, insistence that no children should be selected for admission to the gymnasia until they had completed six years of elementary schooling (the standard Ger-man practice had been that the weeding out process was to take place at the end of the fourth year), and criticism of the ap-prentice system. On the other hand, the principal objective was nevertheless the reform of the German character so as to render it immune to the virus of nazism. Americans believed that the German family was authoritarian, that it was a mistake to segre-gate children in the interests of denominational religious instruc-tion, that the largest possible amount of schooling was desirable, that coeducation should be fostered, and that German teachers should be fashioned into devotees of progressive education doctrine developed in the United States.

It need hardly be indicated that the German who regarded what was being done and said with the requisite measure of seriousness was often more than slightly bewildered. In the first place, he had to reconcile as best he could the very divergent conceptions of what medicine ought to be administered to the fatherland which prevailed among the victorious powers. Second, when he was not a Nazi, and therefore, not committed to the belief that good schooling was a blend of militaristic ballyhoo and *Mein Kampf*, he was likely to feel that his traditional educational system was not inferior to any other, and that indeed it possessed some special merit. We may also properly note that as the war ended the German was quite persuaded that, unless it were true that the German people wholly lacked political ability and sagacity, it could never have put into power a regime which was guilty both of having created death camps like that at Ausschwitz, and of having brought incredible destruction and suffering to the country's cities and towns. The German was accordingly often psychologically prepared to accept the necessity of *Schulreform*. Such preparation was by no means lacking even in the ministries of education, bureaucratic though they might be. But as he became aware of the nature and scope of Occupation plans to alter the character of German schools and universities, he grew increasingly uneasy. And when he then learned of the generalizations which were current among the reformers about the German character and mentality he was often aroused to angry opposition. He had only to look about him in order to observe that the conduct of many who represented the victorious countries was unintelligent and quite immoral. It is not surprising that there should have been formed in the background of his thinking some counter-notions as to how to improve the character of those who, in his opinion, so self-righteously ruled him.

Such was the setting inside which representatives of the United States Government had perforce to carry on. Many of them were able men, and several possessed signal ability. Unfortunately, however, a goodly number were ignorant and mediocre, if not worse. It did not occur to these that any influence they might conceivably exert would depend upon their willingness to learn a little about the character and culture of the people they were supposed to reform. Only a few ventured to make the acquaintance of any Germans. There were officials entrusted with the handling of cultural problems who in seven years never bothered to invite a German to their homes, to look at even the outside of a book published in Germany, or to attend a performance of a German opera or play, excellent though such performances prevailingly were. They sat in their offices and issued orders, frequently reflecting appalling unawareness of the German educational pattern. For these unfortunate aspects of the situation one can blame neither the Army nor the civilian administration which followed it. What was demonstrated must be characterized as the inevitable but saddening discovery that the United States was quite unprepared to take on such complex and truly formidable tasks as both idealism and victory imposed upon it.

In my opinion, which is admittedly retrospective, it would have been far better to send over a few first-rate men and women, to whom there had been allotted freedom to deal with educational and cultural reform in any way upon which they and the emerging pro-democratic Germany could agree. Whenever and wherever this collaboration was attempted by persons equipped to undertake it, the results were astonishingly good. Otherwise the Germans gave in if they were compelled to do so, and then, as soon as they felt the absence of compulsion, went back to their own dear old days with badly concealed jubilation. And for our part, many of us began to entertain serious doubts about the unrestricted rightness of our own views. Not a few thoughtful Americans, having carefully examined the school system established to take care of their own dependent children and having compared the intellectual menu available there with what was served to German youngsters, were tempted to believe that their children were the ones who were faring badly. Then Professor Howard

life which we can endorse all the more heartily because they are born of German tradition and experience. One such idea is that which has established at several universities what is known as the *Studium Generale.* Interested students and professors are banded together within the framework of a residential unit for the purpose of supplementing the specialized training given by the university with courses which promote insight into and discussion of the broader aspects of human culture, so that there will emerge a feeling for the integration of learning. The quality of work done in the *Studium Generale* at such universities as those of Freiburg and Tuebingen is excellent but what impresses one most is the sacrificial willingness of great professors to participate in what is of necessity a pedagogical rather than a research enterprise.

Summing up what has happened since the end of the war, I should say that the results are not spectacular but that they could have been far more meager. We as Americans have talked many things over with other peoples and have concluded that perhaps the mantle of consummate wisdom was not dropped on St. Paul, Minnesota, or Billings, Montana. On the other hand, these have had conversations with us, too, and may have decided that some genuine concern for the advancement of the human spirit is to be encountered even in Spring Hill, Alabama. Today the problem ought not to be whether the inheritors of west European civilization can agree to stop wringing one another's necks, but whether they can in unison bring to the citizen of East Africa or western Asia some assurance that the blessings, however limited, of technology and metaphysical thought will lift the children of those regions above the meager levels of physical and mental subsistence to which they have been inured. In short, if we are wise, we shall see to it that such expedients as the exchange of persons between ourselves and Germany do not flatter mere hedonistic desire to bask in the comforts, aesthetic and culinary, to which our peoples have attained, but are dedicated to the alleviation throughout the vast reaches of mankind of those ills which breed disillusionment and communism.

And so I shall conclude by stressing one lesson which abides with me despite all my awareness of what is wrong with Germany and what, indeed, may be imperfect in this country. It is the realization that great men and women residing in Germany have in many a harvest year gleaned insights into the life of Oriental and African peoples which surpass our own. It seems to me that we might well recruit for service, side by side with our own devoted youth, young German scientists and teachers in order to insure the success of what we too prosaically term the Point IV Program. If they can band together for a task which Albert Schweitzer prophetically envisaged when he deserted the playing of Bach on the great organs of Berlin and which is today the crucial endeavor of mankind, then I predict that there never more will be conflict and the aftermath of devastation to sunder our peoples. Perhaps the deepest sin of the Germans derives from an idealism too easily misled. And no doubt also the supreme temptation of Americans is to forget that one cannot exploit sensibilities without at the same time exploiting human beings.

Destiny, if we heed it aright, has associated us in a common and healing enterprise. When a year ago, I visited the University of Erlangen, I joined for an hour students who were listening to a discourse on Plato. The professor assured his audience that they could follow what he was saying with the aid of a Greek text or a translation. The boy who sat next to me, knowing that I was an American professor, nudged his Greek volume over so that I could read from it too, because he would not have thought it possible that a scholar, which he assumed that I was, could be ignorant of that great tongue. And I confess to a feeling of some pride that for once, at least, I was able to uphold the honor of my country. And so you and I can only hope and believe, for the good of the race to which we belong, that when the peoples share the great sources of their common inspiration they will find a comradeship in action and being which may help to bring us peace.

ACADEMIC FREEDOM*

A DISCUSSION OF ACADEMIC FREEDOM OUGHT TO BEGIN, I THINK,
with an expression of confidence. It seems to me that the temper
of the American people is, in so far as the great issues of personal
liberty are concerned, far better than is often thought. As a
nation we seem to have learned, in the aftermath of many turbulent tides of immigration, that Providence intended ours to be
a society of many divergent and conflicting commitments, uni-
fied by a strong belief in justice for all. That, for example, so
many Americans are earnestly concerned that the Negro should
at last have a chance to walk upward toward the light is surely
a fair sample of the intent of the nation. And so I am persuaded
that we need only offer a workable program for the maintenance
of academic freedom in order to insure adequate support.

Such a program might perhaps stress these convictions:

First, the nation's basic law should embody a clear recognition
of the fact that the Communist party is an aggregation of con-
spirators and their abettors, so that academic adherents to that
party can be dealt with on a basis of clear and well-defined principle rather than of popular sentiment or legal expediency.

Second, the ideological aberrations of "Popular Front" days
should be chalked up to the past, in the reasonable assumption
that by doing so we shall win time for the performance of important tasks as well as for the reconciliation of Americans with
Americans.

Third, every public servant is clearly entitled to do all he can
to expose what he assumes to be subversive influences at work
in American life. The academic fraternity, on the other hand, is

* Reprinted from *The Commonweal* 58 (1953), pp. 11–13.

the sovereign custodian of the laws of evidence, as well as of the principle that the search for truth must be scrupulously exact, undeviatingly objective, and free of personal bias. Whenever it has reason to assume that what is being reported to the people from high places is neither completely fair nor unreservedly correct, it has the right and indeed the solemn duty to call attention to deviations from the established norms of inquiry. Reputable scholarship is the principal source from which criticism derives. It should proceed with firmness, candor, and chilly resolution.

Fourth, the sentiment of the nation might well indicate to the Congress with unmistakable definiteness that an investigation by it of what is taught and by whom would constitute a grave departure from well-established tradition, so long as legislation adequate to deal with subversive movements is not ignored by the academic fraternity.

Fifth, every energy must be mustered to repel incursions by pressure groups into the domain of the schools and colleges, and it is to be insisted upon that only duly constituted boards of trustees and faculties have jurisdiction in this area.

Sixth, academic freedom does not mean that inside the academic community itself any individual can divest himself of the social responsibilty, ethics and courtesy which the profession demands, so that he is at liberty, for example, to attack with vocal prejudice of a narrow and virulent kind the races and religions to which young people belong. It means only that the academic community shall defend the rights of its own individual citizens to free inquiry, to unhampered teaching of subjects controversial or otherwise, and to their views on matters they are competent to discuss.

Seventh, the great texts in which the tradition of academic freedom is enshrined should be studied painstakingly and disseminated as widely as possible, so that the people as a whole may know and understand what is at stake.

Many who profess to favor an inquiry into the university, in all its branches, believe that the detection and exposure of subversives is a proper function of the government, and that therefore the academic profession ought to welcome investigations which will ferret out the guilty. This contention undoubtedly has validity. Agents of subversion are wholly undesirable crows bent on getting into robins' nests on evil missions. But we may surely ask ourselves whether it is advisable to chop down the tree in order to find the crow. It seems to me that certain arguments currently in favor of dismissing adherents of the Communist doctrine from their posts are open to serious question.

For example, it may well be that the Communist is so strongly committed to a view of life that he has lost freedom to think freely. But some will retort that a philosopher who finds all wisdom in Spinoza, or John Dewey, or St. Thomas is also committed to a doctrine and is therefore likewise not free. If one follows such reasoning far enough, one comes to the conclusion, which some unfortunately already endorse, that the only free person is he, who like the nobleman in Chesterton's *Magic*, believes in everything and nothing at the same time.

But if we say that the Communist is, by means of his readiness to conspire against the government and the people of the United States, a clear and present danger, we can safely proceed against him in the light of our traditions. Therewith one enters the realm of law, which is one of the primary concerns of the university, in both a technical and a philosophic sense. And it often sorely troubles responsible educators that, as matters now stand, the law about Communists is nebulous and inchoate. They do not know how to solve puzzles such as this: a teacher can be dismissed from his post for refusing to say whether he has been a Communist, even though it is entirely legal for him to be one. Or again, while a duly established board of inquiry cannot deprive an individual of the right to seek refuge in the Fifth Amendment, the university, as that individual's employer, is expected to do so by ousting him. To many anti-Stalinists on the campus, such procedures seem indefensible; and it may well be as a result that Communists receive a greater measure of sympathy than most of us realize.

These difficulties could be disposed of if the Communist party were declared illegal. For then an academic institution, presented with evidence that a faculty member was guilty, could act promptly and unhesitatingly. It has been argued that the party would go underground if banned. We may properly ask, "Where is it now?" At best such a contention is based on expediency, and here too the end never justifies the means. Banning a political party is, however, not a step to be taken lightly. We might well follow the example of the West German Federal Republic and write into our basic law a constitutional amendment conferring on the Supreme Court authority to decide whether any political organization normally entitled to freedom of speech and assembly constitutes a clear and present danger.

It may be held that these views are too cautious. But as a citizen who had an almost unprecedented opportunity to observe, with horror and loathing, the rise to power in Europe of brutal totalitarian movements, I have become so deeply attached to American traditions of justice and liberty and so wholly persuaded that free institutions crumble because of concessions erroneously made in the name of expediency, that I think the best way to safeguard the American future is to conserve the American past with rigorous care.

If the Communist problem were disposed of, difficulties would remain but not ones of central importance. I have said that the aberrations of "Popular Front" days should be forgotten. During nearly two decades, from the crash of 1929 to the Blockade of Berlin in 1948, the "Front" mustered a great deal of sympathy and support in this country. On many campuses, as in other walks of life, anyone who opposed not the good causes which the "Front" allegedly supported but any political objective of world communism speedily became a pariah. The faithful respected no one's good name, and shied away from no device of dragooning public opinion. As a result, those who were at some time taken in by it are now on the defensive. It is difficult and no doubt often perilous to admit publicly that one contributed, however unwittingly, to the debacle of our civilization. On the other hand, those who were targets during the heyday of amity for sovietism now sometimes take a human, all too human, delight in taunting or exposing their erstwhile tormentors. Some defend Communists out of a probably unconscious desire to rid themselves of blame. Others devote the silence of the night to thanking heaven for Senator McCarthy. The saddening result is that we are not learning in amity what so badly needs to be learned—that emotions, however reputable, are not substitutes for reason and knowledge in human affairs.

We must close that book. And for this reason Senator McCarthy and those who share his purpose are open to serious criticism. But not blind criticism. It is better that the watchdog on the lookout for subversives in government growl too much than that he bark not at all. It is only that the constant opening and shutting of the Pandora's box of moods, convictions, assumptions and slogans which was America in the days when the rest of the world was being carved up by two opposing and equally vicious tyrannies, is an extremely dangerous business from every educational and psychological point of view. For it points the finger of scorn at people who were certainly as well-intentioned as many of their opponents, however mistaken their conception of political reality may have been. The resulting humiliation, agony of spirit and professional debasement which so frequently result are doing the gravest kind of harm to the substance of American life. And consequently I say let us close the box and the book, once and for all, so that we may at length find a way to stand together in what, if we do not so stand, may well be the twilight hour of history.

There is no text in the history of intellectual freedom which should be cited more frequently than that enshrining the words which, according to Plato, Socrates spoke before he died: "No evil can happen to a good man either in life or after death. Wherefore Socrates will not be angry with his condemners, although they meant him anything but good. He will only ask all of them to do to the sons of Socrates what Socrates has done to them." It is from this faith, held sacrificially and resolutely, that the greater part of what is significant and abiding in the tradition of Western thought takes its origin.

Therefore the last (and really also the first) thing to say about academic freedom is that it will endure only as long as those who profess to have a right to it stand ready to pay for it any price which may be exacted. The scholar, the teacher, is one in whom this freedom is incarnate; and as soon as he indicates that he wishes it were not so, or that he would like to go hide under a convenient bushel, there will no longer be a good reason why others should defend the heritage for him. To be sure, silence and a measure of feigned conformity will be necessary under tyranny. Honest men may have to eat the bitter bread of exile in our day. But compromise with evil they dare not.

If in a nation like ours there should exist widespread fear of criticism and much supine acceptance of gags, it might well indicate that many had fallen so deeply in love with security that their sovereign interest was no longer conscience but conformity. Let us hope that this will never be the case. I am not ready to say, as Carl Friedrich does, that the freedom to seek intellectual truth is akin to freedom to profess a religious faith. But certainly these two freedoms have grown up in the same neighborhood. When one is imperiled or corroded, we can be sure that the other is endangered too.

EDITOR'S NOTE: A practical example of Dr. Shuster's attitude toward academic freedom is supplied by the following letter, which he addressed to the Hunter College staff on October 20, 1952:

Certain recent happenings which have resulted from inquiries into subversive activities by Government agencies may well give rise to quite unwarranted fears, and therewith to curtailment of educational activities which must be encouraged if public opinion in the United States is to remain vigorous and forthright. I have some reason to believe that these anxieties are not absent from the campus of Hunter College. This letter is an attempt to clarify the situation.

The character of the Communist Party has led to the passage of legislation designed to curtail its potential influence. Hunter College and its sister institutions are affected in particular by the City Charter, Section 903 of which has been held by the courts to mean that failure to answer questions about membership in the Communist Party when those questions are put by a duly constituted investigative body automatically leads to dismissal from employment by the City. All this has been very well known for some time. The Board of Higher Education could not, even if it desired to do so, disregard this mandate.

There are, however, no laws and no rulings by the Board which constitute any sort of limitation on the non-Communist civic and intellectual interests of the faculty, with this exception: attacks on the race or religion of any student are forbidden. This does not mean that a chance remark or an expression of opinion on a controversial subject will be made an issue. Your College administration will defend to the uttermost any member of the staff from suspicion or retaliation except in those instances in which a chronic seizure of vocal prejudice is indicated.

In every other respect the faculty should not only feel entirely free to act as responsible citizens but, indeed, must be convinced that such conduct is indispensable. When I hear that younger members of the staff, particularly those without tenure, are warned not to act as faculty advisers to student clubs having a political character, I am deeply shocked. No victory the Communist Party could possibly win in this country would be more decisive than would be success in depriving younger instructors of an opportunity to give the leadership which only they can provide. After one has reached a certain age, one acquires for students a manifest august dignity which usually consorts poorly with what they look upon as club life. We must therefore rely on our less venerable colleagues for assistance in this vitally important matter.

Far from gazing upon willingness to share in student enthusiasms and even in student mistakes as an indication of brashness, I am hereby insisting to all Chairmen and Administrative Officers of the College that they look with special benevolence on those members of the staff who do not succumb to current fears but who roll up their sleeves and go to work. Suppose the situation does involve certain dangers. If we can ask a Marine to go up a Korean hill with a grenade in each hand, we can surely expect an instructor in Hunter College not to tremble for the safety of his wife and children if he sits down of an evening and listens to students discuss General Eisenhower or the size of the New York City welfare budget.

I came to Hunter in 1939. Since then I have sometimes been troubled and occasionally annoyed. But nothing that has been said about the College in all these years is more disturbing than are the reports alluded to above. I shall hope they are not true. And I shall look forward to receiving evidence to that effect.

MAN ON THE CAMPUS*

SPINOZA, WRITING TO JELLES, COMMENTED ON A BOOK WHICH seemed to him the "most pernicious" he had ever read. "Money and honors constitute the highest good of the man who wrote it; he inwardly rejects all religion while professing such religion as will best serve to advance him" he concluded. Spinoza's remarks are commonplaces of ethical thought. Socrates and Cicero, Juvenal and Ben Jonson would have been comparably forceful. The "most pernicious" book is unfortunately also a recurring phenomenon. In its most appalling modern version, it is called *Mein Kampf*.

Here is an issue which lends zest and point to the debate about the humanities. It can honestly be said in their behalf that teachers of the literatures and the philosophies have held the things of the spirit, of righteousness, of beauty and honor, in good repute. But we may legitimately wonder whether these teachers have not been woefully complacent about their loyalties—whether the reason why men have listened to other doctrines is not akin to that which keeps them from finding the *summum bonum* in a nightly game of bridge with the rector. Does not the pale cast of boredom too often becloud our concern with the hundred best books, in a world which invites men and women to make books of their own?

Far too frequently we have found vindication of our self-esteem in the theory that, whichever way the fretful midge of opinion might veer, the bright boy in the class would nevertheless some day write a "brilliant" dissertation on the syntax of

* Reprinted from the Winter Number of *The Sewanee Review* (1944), pp. 1–12.

Propertius. Or if his fate was presumed to lie in the pursuit of creative writing, as it is so strangely called, did we not hope that he would always write darkly for "radical" reviews? The chilling fact that nobody reads either dissertations or metaphysical verse out of any motive save devotion to duty did, perhaps, occasionally evoke discomfort. Most of us have, nevertheless, faced the job of what is called "productive scholarship" with a grim determination worthy of the sergeants of Bataan. Even the readers, we find, are sentries sniffing the treason of a confrere's minor errors.

Perhaps the time has come to assume that although dissertations are valuable and pure scholarship a noble ideal, the central humanistic purpose is not implicit in these things. That we need a new definition of what we mean by education is easily and often said. But the validity of every educational ideal depends ultimately upon the validity of the underlying concept of man; and precisely this is difficult to establish in a time as fully committed to philosophic pluralism as is our own. The historian knows that the relative matter-of-factness with which the Middle Ages accepted the Catholic ethical pattern derived from the authority of the Church, which the universities accepted in much the same way as modern schools bow to the inevitability of trustees. German schools and universities became great because of widespread official approval of the Kantian ethic, and of Lutheran reliance upon theological faculties as expounders of sound doctrine. Education as these institutions understood it was, therefore, an august and exacting enterprise, the ultimate objective of which was the fostering of doctrine giving form to the outlook and conduct of the citizen. England, on the other hand, clung for centuries to a pattern of humanistic education based on the code by which the gentleman lived. In these as in other instances, educational effort was consonant with generally agreed upon social and ecclesiastical mores. When these mores were challenged, the schools declined or changed.

Possibly one might argue successfully that the American idea of man likewise served until recently to unify and humanize our educational efforts. Did not the American strive to "take care of himself," even while seeking, eventually, to be of service to society? Self-reliance, not always interpreted in the same manner, was a coveted virtue. Nevertheless, we were always haunted by the dream of a constantly improving, ever more generous, social order to result from the dedication of the individual to the common tasks of the people. Belief in the possibility of progress has been a normal characteristic of the American mind. We as a people would doubtless not have subscribed to the high importance of individual service to society if we had been skeptical of success. This belief in progress must not be interpreted in terms of European philosophy. It has rather been, in the better moments of our history at least, a sort of virtue of hope appended to the virtue of magnanimity. And despite the critics, we did make a good deal of headway. We developed working institutions of republican government. We trusted ourselves with more than a modicum of freedom. And, by and large, we remained generous.

That these social aims sought to find expression in education is obvious. Although from time to time pleas were made for a more epicurean, aesthetic pattern of educated living, the educational leader seldom heeded them. Even today his goal is usually the training of competent individuals possessing social consciences. Much moral philosophy, some of it good and more of it exceedingly bad, has been written from this point of view. One has only to think of the literature of the Progressive Education movement, or of what college presidents said in response to government demands during the present war. Here the tint of pragmatism is often manifest. Pragmatism may well have been an effort to reconcile our realistic pioneering with our ethical worries and social responsibilities. It remains a kind of metaphysics without metaphysical depth of form. To much of what you say in criticism of it I subscribe. But let us remember that it might have been far worse. It might have been something like what one finds in the books of Dietrich Klagges.

Quite evidently, on the other hand, our special American educational assumptions would face a stern test as soon as self-reliance and the social conscience themselves came under attack. The call to battle against both was sounded long ago. Whenever men believed that the "rugged individual" was the kind of person Spinoza castigated, they also began to assert that the social conscience of that individual was no more than a sham. Therewith the pragmatic philosophy could be turned against itself. That philosophy had had a firm puritan core. It assumed a beneficent universe, though it no longer often spoke in terms of the Christian deity. Now, when the critic talked of the individual as *homo rapax*, and of the social conscience as an outmoded prelude to economic engineering, new absolutes were projected in relation to which the single person envisaged by the pragmatists was considered scarcely more than an acquiescent automaton. At the present moment, the schools are still firmly on the side of tradition. But they are troubled. They have even discovered within themselves habits of shoddy compromise and debilitating superficiality.

To some extent, no doubt, the mass education project to which our schools have been dedicated secrets its own corrosive bile. Toynbee's well-known comment on yellow journalism as the immediate consequence of the Education Act of 1870 illustrates the complexity of the problem. If the schools are coveted because of the assumption that learning is economically advantageous, popular demand will inevitably insist that the assumption be proved not illusory. And as a matter of fact many educators have tried hard to demonstrate, from *Who's Who* and other sources, that college is actually an open sesame to a larger income. Much more regrettable, however, is the interpretation of the school as a begetter of hedonistic satisfaction. Of course no one will deny that intellectual pleasure is a good, or that reading has a certain value when it is used only to while away the time. But when reading is little more than indulgence in sensations which are experiments in vicarious physical guzzling, the question whether it is not actually baneful must be put in dead earnest.

It is now impossible to ignore the fact that the average college graduate differs little, in so far as his intellectual attitudes are concerned, from the mass of Americans. Knowledge of what the alumnus reads is sickening. And that this surrender to hedonism involves of necessity the repudiation of intelligence as a social instrument is clear from a hundred examples. One must suffice. When this war began, it was widely asserted that the American people were not prepared to face their desperate plight because "the colleges" had failed to teach the truth about contemporary problems and events. Mr. Paul V. McNutt repeated the charge at a meeting of the American Association of Colleges shortly after Pearl Harbor. As a matter of fact, our best teachers did their utmost to oppose the partisan and often poorly informed journalism which after 1918 weaned the citizen from realism. But those teachers had no influence. Hayes, Seymour, Wright, and the others had a total audience only a fraction of the size of that which read the comments of Mr. Earl Browder. Mr. McNutt obviously had never heard of them. How could these things have happened if the American college graduate read books having an intellectual density greater than that of *If Winter Comes?*

That being the situation, it will not do to assume that anything short of radical reform of the underlying educational ideal can "save the humanities." I for one am not interested in saving them if they cannot save themselves. Expedients can, to be sure, garner a few plums. By compressing the "general education" given by the colleges into the first two years, and by a judicious modification of the requirements for the professional studies, one can compel students to absorb a certain amount of English, history, mathematics and philosophy. Of what earthly use is this compulsion if it does not help the student to discover and satisfy a vital need? On the other hand, it is equally evident that one must not erect barriers which automatically prevent the majority of students from getting some humanistic education. Such barriers are, for instance, raised by faculties which insist that all vocational training is incompatible with the "liberal" purpose of the college. Students do not want to find themselves, at the end of four years, totally unprepared to begin any practical task. They are correct in this negative position. I conclude, therefore, that wise and cautious educational planning is valuable, but that it alone will not suffice.

Radical reform cannot be effected through recourse to other educational patterns than those Americans have known. We are what we have been, for better or for worse. Attempts to transform us into Germans, Frenchmen, or medieval Catholics may be picturesque, but they will never be anything else. Going back therefore to the formula of self-reliant individual and social conscience, let us see what can be done, not out of a salesman-like assumption that our American experience is peculiarly sacred, but out of a deep conviction that it is all we have to work with because it is all that we are. Well, what is wrong is, first of all, the absence of what Unamuno called the "tragic sense of life." We have come to take it for granted that there is a remedy for every ill. New drugs will cure ancient diseases. Victories which are followed by the hanging of a Mussolini will usher in brave newer worlds. Nature is beneficent—a storehouse of vitamins and energy, which the inventive genius of man will render more and more subservient. And so on.

It would be disastrous enough if only the yellow journal and the radio advertiser enunciated these fallacies. When one realizes that the American college itself far too frequently preaches the same false doctrine, one has reason for profound alarm. For the terrible truth is that the "self-reliant" modern individual is weirdly unhappy. No gadget will relieve anguish and loneliness of the spirit, curb the suffering caused by the decline of physical beauty when that is the only good, or leave the wife who is mistress solely less distraught when a new mistress appears. All the psychiatrists available cannot dam the mounting torrent of agony that gushes from the flagrant contradiction between our current assumptions of infinite optimism and the laws, or the facts, of psychic life. Sometimes the welled-up misery explodes in the horrible grimace of some tragedy of degradation. But it mounts everywhere behind the façade of our collective life, a bitter and poignant hunger and thirst, an erosion of the last supports of the heart of man, an acid poured into the flesh of the ultimate human *Ding-an-sich*.

And the social conscience? I lived in Germany during the critical years during which nazism grew strong. It is safe to say that there was then less misery in the country than there had been even in the years prior to 1914. But there was none of what is termed "security," by which I mean not social insurance but rather a feeling that one could follow any pursuit with relative assurance of lasting freedom to continue. New economic phenomena—inflation, taxation—had demonstrated the precariousness of all reserve financial strength. And beyond that, new forms of mass psychosis had frightened the individual into believing that unless he was in rapport with the dominant psychosis he could not survive. Healthier societies than the German may muster energy to counteract these terrors. They are, nevertheless, part and parcel of modern life as such, and they have poisoned more than the air even in America. For how can the social conscience function unless it feels that the forces against which it contends are not overwhelming the individual man? One has only to compare older expressions of the American mind in such books as those of Miss Addams and Mrs. Dorr with, say, the writings of Mr. Burnham to see what is meant. If social betterment is a problem in engineering, why should one expect anything to matter save the discovering of the efficient engineer?

Surely we cannot go on assuming that life is all rainbows and nature a fairy godmother if we are no longer certain that as individuals we can do something about either. What can save us from the craze of fear is, therefore, only a restatement of our ideals in terms of cosmic reality. We have to understand our weakness and our tragedy in order to realize our strength. Personally, I do not think that this understanding is possible without theism and all that it implies. A humanism which assumes permanent values without positing Permanent Value seems to me to be aping a player who moves chessmen about a board without realizing that there is such a thing as a game of chess. I shall not argue the matter further, because obviously American education is not yet in a mood to look upon a discussion of theism as an issue of practical moment. We shall merely take it for granted, as was done at the outset, that the humanities are concerned with values, and that a value is a good as distinguished by the informed conscience from an evil. If these values can make the individual inwardly self-reliant—instead of merely self-reliant in terms of monetary or power success,—then we may hope, with Spinoza, for a restoration of moral balance.

To speak of values at all is to assume as an indispensable prelude the validity of means employed in the discovery of values. That is, we must believe in language, in thought, and in moral discernment as aspects of character-forming method. We shall not merely counsel students to learn how to write short stories that will earn money, but we will also tell them that communication is the individual's sole route of discovery. We shall not discuss the laws of thought as techniques helpful in making friends and influencing people, for that is the manner in which the Sophists discussed them; but we shall talk about them as matters even more vital than the laws of hygiene and physics. We shall ban relativism as if it were the plague, and insist that discernment of the good has been the rigorous business of all the rigorous philosophies. I should say that this hard work is more precious even than is concern with the world's great thinkers and writers. It is not a hundred books which matter, but rather how to grow intellectually while reading a book. Youth simply cannot have too much of what the French call *explication de texte*, or what the old schoolmen called logic. Asking them to read Kant and Aquinas before they have known these things is like asking a boy to play a Bach toccata before he has learned his scales.

That is why, incidentally, the American system of vacations is excellent, provided it is properly utilized. Young men who work during the summers come to know the speech of common men, in which there is little learning but often much of shrewd, hard common sense. They drop the habit of exclusive association with abstractions, which is the inevitable characteristic of formal academic study, for a useful time, returning to it with mingled

humility and realism. The four-quarter college is an act of surrender to bookishness from which no possible good can come.
On the other hand, collegiate loafing during three months of
summer, on the theory that young people need a rest, is a shocking concession to false gods. It will never do any young person
harm to mingle with farmers and laborers, artisans and sportsmen.
What does matter incalculably is the concession to hedonism
which is implicit in leisure at a time when leisure is not necessary.

There will come an hour, sooner or later, when the young mind
will begin to explore down alluring intellectual paths. Then he
must have all possible freedom. The moment will have come to
loosen the bond of formal requirement and of pedagogical inter-
ference. The good college is one whose teachers will sense in-
tuitively that their student is at the beginning of this journey,
and will make available encouragement and stimulus, guidance
and bluff comment, as required. Whether you call the result of
such intuition the "honors system" or not is an item of no consequence. "Honors" can be as bald and unproductive as any other
of a dozen educational methods if improperly managed. And I
make bold to say that failure is principally due to the fact that as
teachers we do not light the way to any future conceivable to a
young mind. The scholar, doomed to his research within the narrow limits of his specialization, prides himself on talking to none
save his equals. But your boy must live among men. Therefore,
what you really want is not the bright lad's eventual thesis on
Propertius's syntax, but his self-reliance and his conscience. We
have got, therefore, to get these scholars of ours out among men.
May the time come when they stand at street corners as Francis
and Bernard stood at the crossroads; when they go into prisons
and countinghouses; and when they share in every civic effort!

Above all, we do not want a dismal college, with impossible
standards of achievement. What matters is, after all, not so much
whether a young man does what he is told by his elders as
whether he does what he is told by his own best self to do. Once
I had a student who was asked to compete for the honor of writing a class ode. He submitted a sonnet, which had to be rejected

because it was that. Nevertheless, it was a good sonnet, which I included years later in an anthology, from which it has been quoted widely. Therefore, I say let there be discipline but also laughter—that laughter in company which, as Bergson wrote, makes community. One must also not be chary of games, unless they become pageants which gamble for huge sums and pander incidentally to the worst instincts of the crowd. Let your college be as human as the word humanities implies.

It seems to me, then, that we can send the American people off thirsting for the "liberal arts" if we tell them the truth about themselves and about ourselves. That truth will hurt, as truth has always hurt. But unless it is preached with sincerity and sacrifice, the triumph of vapidity will be followed by the victory of social dissolution. The modern individual simply cannot stand on the creaking floor now under his feet. To tell him that he will have a private airplane, or sit on a plastic chair, or live in a prefabricated house, may amuse him for a time, or even keep him gainfully employed. But he is not a motor, nor is he made of lucite, nor can he dodge the difficult business of shaping his own life. For heaven's sake, let us not say to him that together with these marvels he will have a great deal of leisure which he can devote to Milton and Shakespeare. Let us tell him in words which he can understand that the house of his soul will tumble in a heap about him unless he builds it aright. And having said that as earnestly as we know how, let us get back to work. It is a big job we have to perform. It is to defeat the principalities and the powers which are, without realizing it, drying up the substance of American life.

TO THE FRESHMEN
OF HUNTER COLLEGE: I*

THE PLEASANT CHORE GIVEN ME TODAY IS NOT MERELY TO WEL-
come you to the college, which we of the faculty do with cordial
sincerity, but to explain as painlessly as possible what it means
that you have come. You are in the main children of New York,
accustomed to school-going, who would doubtless be greatly
astonished if the process stopped at the close of twelve years.
Yet not too long ago higher education was in this country as
elsewhere the concern of very few. Most of them were the
sons and daughters of parents professionally committed to well-
established forms of intellectual living. They were ministers of the
Gospel, rabbis, professional men, teachers, and poets. It was often
considered beneath the dignity of the materially successful to
suppose that higher education could be of use to their children,
even if upon occasion unruly temperaments were temporarily
and partially laid to rest on the bosoms of distinguished alma
maters. That is the major reason why so many eminent Americans, Abraham Lincoln in the vanguard of them, taught themselves beside log fires or more advanced methods of illumination.
In the present hour we Americans believe that as many people as
are at all qualified should go to college. The precentage of those
who do has almost doubled within a generation, and there is every
prospect that it will rise even further.

But it is probably true that the number of young people who
are soundly trained in what we call the liberal arts is, percentage-
wise, not larger than it was when the twentieth century dawned.

* Delivered at a freshman convocation in September 1956.

This is explained by the fact that vocational purposes and objectives have, as the mighty tide of students rolled upon the college beach, almost automatically come into the foreground. For by reason of economic circumstance and other factors boys and girls have had to think largely of what they were going to do after graduation in order to earn a livelihood. And so there has come to be a form of educational engineering or planning which uses a professional course of study as a base and tries then to insert liberal arts subjects into such nooks and crannies as can be found. Sometimes this method works rather well. Often it fails to do so.

Hunter College does not subscribe to such a plan. Since it is a college of the liberal arts, I should perhaps indicate briefly what these are. They are studies, of language and literature, of mathematics and the sciences, of history and of the notable forms of social behavior—psychological, political, economic, sociological, anthropological, which if carefully pursued provide basic information, instruct in accuracy of thought and expression, and form judgment. With them the noble arts of music, painting, and sculpture are associated as forms of literature having their own lofty and distinctive being. We say not only that these constitute our legacy of human culture, but also that they are means through the use of which any one of us may attain unto a measure of personal cultivation. And as a consequence at Hunter professional or vocational training is fitted into a liberal arts course of study. This training is what I have sometimes called an "inlay." For example, though a great many teachers are prepared here for vocations in institutions ranging all the way from the nursery school to the high school, nobody majors in educational methods. This does not mean that they are poorly prepared. On the contrary, I believe I may say that our graduates have given a good account of themselves, indeed.

Now one must perforce proceed to say that a liberal education is at bottom impossible to define—that it is rather an experience to be lived through, a banquet that is served, a journey entered upon and only in a certain sense completed. And whichever of these metaphors you prefer, the heart of the matter is the association between student and professor. I think therefore that the best way in which I can explain to you in advance what college life is and ought to be is by introducing you to a teacher. The portrait is, to be sure, a composite one. That is, I have not singled anybody out and have above all tried to avoid anything that might suggest Mr. Chips.

Sometime during the teens a young man or woman suddenly becomes aware of the flavor of the intellectual life. I think that hour dawns relatively early. One may be fifteen or nineteen. The sap of the soul rises then to the topmost branches which have a clear view of the sky and which therefore yearn to leap up toward the sun, as we have all seen the tips of the young hawthorn do in the spring. Only that this great new realm which opens to the spirit in a flash happens to be, though not devoid of shout and sign and color, compounded—this can only be phrased awkwardly, hesitatingly—of vision rather than of visibilities. Many great poets have talked retrospectively of it. Keats opened Chapman's *Homer*. Newman writes, "When I was fifteen (in the autumn of 1816) a great change of thought took place in me." Very often there is an element of moral decision in this awareness, sometimes stern and even extravagant. We read that the boy Carlyle, having quarreled with his brother over a game of cards, threw the deck into the fire as if it were a resource of Satan and never played again.

I stress the element of moral decision because if the moment of initial vision is to flower into a life of scholarship the discipline to which the conscience thenceforth subjects itself must remain unflagging. One cannot honestly or successfully live the life of the mind unless one is committed wholeheartedly to what is true and what is free. Of course the young person I have described will not immediately know how to proceed on his own momentum. Always there is the great book, the great teacher, the stimulating if also exacting companion. And so from the very outset of the scholar's life, teaching and learning are combined. No doubt relatively few of those who respond to the hour of insight indicated actually think immediately of an academic career. There is part of a poet in every worthy scholar, something of an artist, often a bit of a prophet and reformer. It is only gradually that the example of great teachers suggests a life pattern, presses him into the mold of what we call, for lack of a better term, the profession.

Now I think one of the greatest difficulties in this development is that at the beginning a young person sees, dimly it is true but nevertheless sharply, the whole—that is all the things there are to learn, all the things which one might be. The boy or girl is growing biologically and socially as well as intellectually. The desire to be in love and in the library at the same time is eminently natural. And to span the wide arc which stretches from language to philosophy, from economics to sculpture, seems the only logical thing to do. These impulses are sound and the business of a good college is to cultivate even while pruning them. There must be time for warmhearted affection, for games, even for trying out one's wits and feet on the dance floor. And scholastically speaking the course of study does the best that can be done to satisfy the craving for universality by letting the students see something, in a reasonably integrated way, of all the major arts and sciences.

But then comes the hour when the young person destined to be a teacher and scholar chooses. Will he be historian or mathematician, anthropologist or devotee of the French language and literature? This decision is seldom an easy one. It is in part based on discovered aptitudes and on a kind of vocation. But it is likely to be the result also—in many cases primarily the result—of the impact left by virile and inspiring teachers. Then at the end of the college period there comes the cold, often dank and foggy hour in which one must make up one's mind to throw away the allurements of the moment—the job and what it will win, the allurements of freedom—and decide to take the long, hard road of the disciplined scholar. Make no mistake. It is paved with cobblestones and the feet of the walker are often very sore. Getting the doctor's degree means carrying during interminable hours a heavy baggage of books, means standing at attention when one would far rather slouch, means never being quite sure the long trek will ever come to a successful end. The captains of this army are exacting. Then, unless one happens to be extremely fortunate, there are all sorts of KP duties to perform. Apprentice teaching, for example, done for a pittance, often under conditions akin to peonage, under the keen eye of supervisors ruthless in their judgment.

That there are men and women who break under all this is no secret. But those who reach the end of this novitiate successfully have another ordeal to face. Each one is a member of a group, sometimes large, of persons interviewed by departments in institutions they have never seen before. It is like running a gauntlet where one's intellectual muscles are felt to see if they are sound, and where the elusive thing known as one's personality is sampled as if it were a wine. There follows the period of probation, during which the individual never knows what the final judgment passed on him will be. It all sounds rather terrible, and it is, but this is the way it should be. The responsibility for living the intellectual life freely and fully, and for the formation of young minds, is one of the four basic responsibilities upon which the vitality of our nation ultimately rests. The others are responsibility for spiritual welfare, for health, and for government.

And what a glorious achievement it is to emerge in the end the scholar as Emerson saw him, free and brave, aware of vistas which are more endless even than landscapes of mountains and seas, cheerfully and humbly aware of one's very finite limitations in relation to the potential infinity of knowledge, and yet to be with every fiber of one's being a teacher as well, enamored of the dialogue between youth and age which is the central business of the college, having malice toward none and charity for all. To sense as one grows older the magnanimity of one's calling, never if one can help it to let a young person down—to know through wise experience what are the woes as well as the ecstasies of adolescence, and through the impact of these insights to avoid any stiffness in one's own aging. And to sense finally, in quiet hours, the tinge of holiness which is inseparable from all this, that insight into the fact that, as à Kempis wrote, *magna res est amor*, a mighty thing is love even when experienced only through analogy.

All that I can really tell you about college is that you will have four years during which to be with, talk with, listen to, study under men and women of this character. The memory of some of them will be inseparable from the rest of your lives. Few of you will go on to become scholars and teachers in the sense described. You will for the most part stop at the end of four years and take up your share of the world's work. You will have your babies or your careers. But I trust we shall, God willing, be able to give you a light for the long path which will never go out again. Remember, you are not here to be thrilled or soothed, coddled or cajoled. To us you come as young friends, each with his own ability and desires, expected to stand on your own feet and ask for help if you cannot. We shall treat you neither as mama's darlings nor as waifs. But I who am the president of the college say at the outset what the members of the faculty would themselves never say—here are the best teachers we could find for you, put your hands in theirs proudly and confidently, for this is as noble a college as the land affords. And I say to the faculty also, with gratitude to them for having come today, that this is also an hour when we might well think with renewed affirmation of that dedication of heart and mind which we first vowed when we girt our loins, took staffs in our hands, and started out on the starlit road.

TO THE FRESHMEN
OF HUNTER COLLEGE: II*

THE WELCOME WE ARE GIVING YOU TODAY IS RATHER SPECIAL AND
solemn. We of the faculty are arrayed in gowns, hoods and
caps which, however uncomfortable they may be, have a distinguished pedigree, linking us of the present with scholars of
the great universities and colleges of medieval Europe. It is also
surmised that, unlike the restless part of the audience which in
Shakespeare's time witnessed *The Merchant of Venice*, you have
music in your souls. Accordingly, we are offering you some.
And of course there must be an address. The occupational diseases of college presidents are several, but first on the list is
oratory. This I shall now proceed to reveal in all its dire malig-
nancy.

We shall discuss the setting in which a college student is presumed to be the jewel. It is a topic which no one familiar with the
American tradition can talk about without a measure of nostalgia,
grateful for progress though he may be. Our colleges of yore,
more than faithful to their Cambridge ancestry, used to be places,
rural if at all possible, wherein young men or women were duly
cloistered for the school year. One seldom left the premises, except for the long summer vacations. Persons of the opposite sex
were dreamed of, carried about in photographic effigies, and
upon occasion wooed in amorous epistles. But they were rarely
seen. The objective was comradeship, confraternity, between
young people and instructors for the business of learning. But
above all there was the community of students, of which New-

* Delivered at a freshman convocation in September 1957.

47

man wrote almost ecstatically, against the background of Oxford, busy with talk and games both grave and gay.

Such colleges are all but things of the past. Even the rural campus, however encrusted with ivy it may be, empties of week ends as do New York office buildings. Or if its inmates be males, the college is inundated with Sabbath Eve regularity by waves of parents, relatives, and above all, girl friends, real or prospective. And of course a modern urban institution like ours, whether on Park Avenue or in the Bronx, tends to be one in which no man or woman hath an abiding place. Yet we all pay tribute to our memories, real or fancied, of the college that used to be.

We too wish to create a community, a comradeship. It is imperative that we should. Much is written about youth, delinquent or otherwise. I shall quote a rather significant comment on this elusive subject, from a recent book by Richard Vincent McCann:

> The adolescent may find that the conduct which seems to be expected of him by the individuals and institutions representing authority, or by the adult world in general, would require him to be someone that he simply cannot conceive of himself as being. This is largely due to the fact that he cannot conceive of himself at all.

I have no doubt that this is often true. And if it is, the college should first of all be a place in which a young person finds out how to see, to conceive of, himself. Only then can he go on to fit that concept into the community of which he has become a part. This sounds quite simple but naturally it is not. Human beings, modern human beings in particular, can be very lonely. And if they are, all sorts of suggestions as to how the chill bonds of isolation can be broken will crop up out of their subconscious minds. Some people rush, for instance, into ill-considered romantic love affairs, in the delusion that through them escape into comradeship can be found. But, alas, nothing in the world is more harrowingly empty than is the bitter end of ephemeral romance. How many times since the days of acrid little Madame Bovary has that been tragically discerned! Or, to take something notably different, one may immure oneself in the world of books. These can be hugged to oneself, they cannot run away. Their substance is poured out at the reader's command. Yet useful, companionable, though books may be, they can lock us behind their doors and put the keys in their pockets.

The college will not automatically make the discovery of the valid self for anybody. It is only the laboratory, even if the attractive laboratory, in which each one must seek his own results through his own experiments. Of course your elders will prod and guide, and they have learned a good many new things about the "self" in general. It is an area in which it is folly not to be as wise as possible. But regrettably enough the lore will not assist us too much as individuals. I am afraid that the great American pastime of self-psychoanalysis can never prove to be more than a rather morose and murky variety of solitaire.

Yet there are a few things we might note as points of profitable departure. First, we mortal beings are, strange though it seem, free. However strongly felt the influences of heredity and environment may be, most of us do possess the sovereign liberty of choice, of making decisions, rightly or wrongly, for good or evil. This fact could be ignored for a long while but it cannot be henceforth. What a strange world it now seems once to have been—with a theory of civil liberties which insisted that all of us must be free and at the same time with an underlying doctrine of determinism which held that none of us could do anything of his sovereign will. We now know, for example, that we are at liberty to concern ourselves with the great ultimate problems of human destiny, or to restrict our thought to whatever can be immediately useful. Nothing ingrained in our blood streams makes this decision for us, any more than brutal tyrants *had to* destroy six million people in the gas ovens of Belsen and Auschwitz, or *had to* suppress a Hungarian uprising in blood.

It follows, then, that we are free to appraise ourselves, to explore the major contours of our complexity. The young lady of long ago who, having been told by an adoring swain that she was beautiful, thanked God that love is blind, had been looking in the mirror. Why not be just as realistic about the rest of ourselves? What is there to be said in our favor? And what by way of indictment? Andrew Marvell said of Charles II on the scaffold that

> He nothing common did or mean
> Upon that memorable scene.

At seventeen or eighteen the scene of life is already memorable. To have integrity of self is the prelude to generosity unto others. But there can be no integrity that is not based on an honest inventory. It is my belief that most young people like you are likely to underestimate your abilities rather than to over-assess them, while at the same time placing too high a value on your qualities of character. Why not recall that your minds will never again be as keen as they are at twenty . . . and remember that you cannot be responsible for what you do with that sharp-edged sword any other time than now. Twenty years hence your regrets will be as out of date as powdered wigs.

The college offers you several devices of use in making a continuing inventory of yourselves. The first is inevitably what happens through the course of study. Here a student, confronted with requirements, is likely to mutter against the world of his masters and say, "On what compulsion must I?" This enforced compliance may, it is true, be irrational upon occasion. No one knows better than do I that not all academic requirements make sense. But looking back on the history of the principal plan devised to offset them—the honors system—I believe that it never has amounted to much more than a means of assigning fewer students to a teacher than would othewise be the case. When the honors system has succeeded, it is because the requirements it imposed were more exacting, however less formal, than otherwise. The teacher who does not demand his pound of flesh from his students also makes no loan of intellectual money.

The second device is that of discussion. This is the anvil on which a college community is forged. Here the "I" and the

"Thou" emerge, as Martin Buber has indicated. In the discovery of the "Thou" by the "I" the second is revealed as it could not otherwise be. The temper of a campus can be judged only by the vitality and breadth of the discussion which takes place on it. No doubt one like ours is always imperiled by the disparity of the surrounding culture, which in turn forces the monologue to the center of the stage. We see, listen to, so many professionals of the stage, screen, television, sports, that we tend to assume that somebody else can manage intellectual discourse for us. No doubt somebody always does know more about something than do we. But we never really learn to any other tune than talking. What would literature be if we stripped it of the great books of dialogue—Plato, the Talmud, the Gospels, the *Summa* of St. Thomas, or indeed almost all significant modern drama? Who, for example, would read Shaw just for his prefaces? But who that considers his plays for what they are, namely scintillant discussion, can let them be? Certainly a good college, whatever measure of room it finds for the monologue—which is the lecture —has no mind-forming character-building device to compare with the discussion into which you can enter with your instructors and your fellows. You may have to listen to quite a bit of nonsense—even Socrates did—and you will no doubt contribute some of your own. But you will in the end acquire the art of giving form to your thought while discovering the infinite diversity and meaningfulness of other people.

There is much else to be said about forming a college community which we cannot consider today. There is, for example, work experience, which for a student comes from participating in the tasks that help build our common life—the activities of Student Council, of the theatrical and musical organizations, of clubs and comparable groups. But it does seem wise to remind ourselves, whether we be the masters of the college or its young people, of what it ultimately is to which we aspire. Let me reminisce a bit, as is the fateful privilege of older men. During the First World War I was sent to join a small band of French soldiers at the Front, engaged during the dirty and difficult business of trench warfare in trying to pick up telephone conversations.

One night as we sat under hours of heavy bombardment in a dugout lighted by candles, I started to read a stray volume of Carlton Hayes's *European History* picked up somewhere, only to note that the older French soldier beside me took from his pocket a volume of Aeschylus in Greek. This he carried with him always; and I recall being humble at the thought that this man, who had survived four years of awful carnage, could still light his spirit by the fire of that great verse. I felt certain then that the true measure of education was just this—that it could give a human being for all his life, regardless of the circumstances in which it had to be lived, imperishable love for great art, great truth and for profound spiritual insight. I now reckon that soldier among my best teachers. The next morning when the bombardment was ended we went out to repair our lines and found the body of a young *poilu*, pathetically young it seems to me now, lying with a bullet through his head. We carried his broken body back on a plot of grass, and looked to see who he might have been. In his pocket was a letter written but not mailed to a girl in the south of France. Filled it was with the song and flowers of his little town, written with a beauty akin to that of a melody in Arcady. I sensed then that it is never very far from life sensitively lived, in the spirit of a noble folk tradition, to the great verse of antiquity—that the second always keeps a way of seeping through a culture, provided the men and women who know it never sell their heritage for a mess of pottage but let it shine through their lives as the lamp of which the Greeks also spoke— the lamp which, taking, we light the way for each other.

What if college life can be for us that kind of enterprise? We are privileged to sit at a great window looking at the ever-changing, yet essentially unchanging panorama of the past as it moves by in the interweaving configurations of science, thought, poetry, art, contemplation, rising then with the reflection of these upon our spirits, to go on our way again with hope for the race to which we belong, with kindness, and possessing an inward peace so virile that its contagion will affect the greater community to which we shall be bound during our days on the earth. We shall wish for you and for ourselves that it may be so.

EDUCATION
AND WISDOM*

THE SUBJECT THAT THIS MODEST ESSAY WILL DEAL WITH HAS AS
many branches as a tall tree. I shall treat a few of them. First
of all, contemporary America fosters a great deal of scholarly
inquiry, and likewise supports a tremendous educational enterprise. Our learned societies have become mass movements. Chemists meeting in conclave can fill Atlantic City to the brim. The
modern languages are served by an association of more than six
thousand members, who annually produce a program of addresses
so complex in character that no one can absorb more than a small
part of it. Even musicology and aesthetics, relatively new disciplines in this country, are already evoking so many scholarly
papers and monographs that it would be difficult for hard-working specialists to evaluate what is being written. On the teaching
side, the major groups of educators resemble vast and powerful
unions. They have made the business of tests and measurements
a big business, indeed, and when they discuss pedagogical methods
they revel in a professional jargon of which the average citizen
can make neither head nor tail.

Here then are two mastodons, and one cannot say that much
love is lost between them. Merely to suggest to a scholar who
teaches at a college or in a university that possibly the specialist
in educational arts might tell him something interesting about
how to give instruction is to run the risk of assassination. I have
tried it. On the other hand, the American schoolteacher is, when
measured by the norms of contemporary scholarship, endowed

* Reprinted from *The Commonweal* 50 (1949), pp. 36–45.

with what might be termed a mid-nineteenth century mentality. He doesn't see scholarly publications in his field, his general reading habits are depressing, and his genuine idealism may be coated with lavender and old lace. It seems to me that he does a better job of teaching than his university colleague (exceptions having been duly noted), but there is reason to fear that what he teaches may be thin and seriously out of date.

Much of all this is human and unavoidable. The mere thought that elementary schoolteachers might ask for time off in order to do research sends shivers up and down the spine, and I shall confess that I cannot think of the Harvard graduate faculty taking instruction in pedagogy without a chuckle. Nevertheless one will hardly escape feeling that the fragmentation of learning and education is one key to the dishevelment of the contemporary mind. If we cannot even put together what we know and what we say inside the school system, how shall we ever transfer what we know to our common life? To be sure, much of what is called research probably isn't of breath-taking importance. The world may well get on even if a dozen texts edited by the Arabic Society are never read, though one can't be too cocksure. But a great deal is vital, indeed. How shall we get it into our veins? The ideological naïveté of the American during the past twenty years has had the most appalling consequences. That naïveté seems to me to spring less from malformation of our moral and intellectual norms than from a most distressing untidiness of mind. We are like children who have been given puzzles so large that we cannot sort out the pieces.

I think it may help us to try for the nonce to stand far enough away from what we are doing to enable us to see it in perspective. It may not be necessary, though it would be desirable, to view the scene against the background of eternity. Surely it will do no harm to use a telephoto lens. I trust therefore that you will forgive my making at this point a bow in the direction of antiquity, by which I mean the culture slowly fashioned by mankind prior to the age of modern nationalism. For this present age has a character peculiarly its own. Nations as we know them have

possessed great cultural vitality and initiative, but their protagonists can fairly be accused of having coated the human mind
with armor plate—that is of having more or less subtly and
imaginatively subjected the quest for truth to the quest for
power. Almost every European nation has created a great literature, a very influential philosophy, and a noble art; but in general these things have been used, often most unwisely, for the
sake of the "national culture" which produced them. While
making a study of Germany's eastern boundary in the year 1930,
for example, I was taken first by Germans and then by Poles to
view the sites of ancient towns which, each group contended,
demonstrated beyond the shadow of a doubt the identity of the
"national stock" which had originally settled the region. Whether
the minster of Strasbourg (or should one write Strassburg)
ought to be looked upon as a French or a German masterpiece
is again a problem which has whetted the appetite of many a
writer.

It may be argued on the other hand that antiquity, circum-
scribed though it may have been by the special concerns of
regions and empires, was by comparison devoted to matters of
universal cultural import. The Old Testament is a book about
God and the people He chose. Yet it is certainly no propagandis-
tic essay in behalf of that people, being as much a treatise on
Jewish, or human, defection from high principle as it is an account of Jewish knowledge of and obedience to the divine Law.
The Romans, for their part, lived in constant awe of the Greek
mind. Catullus copied Theocritus and Vergil, Homer. Yet the
Greeks in their turn had unflaggingly looked eastward. And of
the Christian empire which succeeded that of the Caesars, one
may say that Alfred and Charlemagne foreshadowed in their efforts to foster learning the inevitability of Aquinas's restatement
of the Aristotelian philosophy.

At all events, I suspect that the principal reason why we are
dissatisfied with the present state of learning, as that is dispensed
through what we are pleased to call "education," is this: We
have now come to the place where we can see the compromises

of pragmatism, in particular of nationalistic pragmatism, as clearly as a park patrol can see the vestiges of picnics on a Monday morning. We know that man has compelled truth to serve his practical purpose, and we are as a result distressed. Matters may not have been too bad while there was an Italian point of view, or an English way of doing things, or even a Russian Messianism. Now, however, with a fatefulness that would be farcical if it were not so alarming, the nations themselves have in many instances been cut up into partisan, mutually destructive bands of pragmatists, and it is apparent that "we moderns"—whoever we may be—are no longer talking the same language or going to the same places. And when the confusion of tongues becomes so loud that no one can hear what is being said, we cease, of course, to have learning or education as we desire to have them.

Accordingly no great harm will be done by positing, for consideration if not emulation, the relative unity of antique civilization. The man of antiquity seems to have conceived of education in several ways. For one thing, he dealt with the practical arts in a quite nonacademic manner. Despite the fact that the Romans were magnificent engineers who built viaducts and roads, towns and fortresses, with a skill which still earns our unstinted admiration, and despite the circumstance that such natural sciences as mathematics, physics and even chemistry were pretty far advanced in their time, it is impossible to discover traces of any school to which Roman engineers were sent. Quite as remarkable is the fact that such gifted architects as he who drew the plans for the amphitheater of Trier apparently never earned any sort of degree. We can only conclude that the great empire relied on a system of apprenticeship as difficult to reconstruct as it must have been efficient. On the other hand, a slight acquaintance with Cicero will indicate that the pursuit of the highest art, namely wisdom, was, though begun early in the schools of rhetoric, really the concern of men who had profited by wide experience. Cicero's greatest heir, Augustine, tells us that he began his quest for wisdom at the "age of nineteen," but it is not an anomaly that he really got down to it when he was a mature man.

What the schools of rhetoric accomplished was to start young men on their way. It was only when some of the best among them had a chance to do what Cicero did, and settle down to the task of reconciling their experience among men with their reflections on the meaning of life, that something solid and substantial was accomplished.

Education of the formal sort, therefore, had precious little to do with the unity of antique civilization. The majority of the teachers appear to have been rather adept at starting discussion, commenting on texts, and propounding scintillating theories of their own. But there seems to have been little solidarity among them. The greatest revolution which occurred in Greek educational history started when a veteran named Socrates came home from the wars. The kind of question he asked was highly disturbing to classroom routine because it was really based on a deep and vital concern with truth. He would not be put off with stock phrases or rule-of-thumb evasions. He gave some of his fellow students an inkling of the meaning life might have for them by appealing to the moral sense, or conscience, of man. And though he ran afoul of prevailing Greek opinion, he prepared the way for Plato and Aristotle, and therewith for all those for whom Greek culture holds deep meaning today.

The unity of the ancient world, therefore, was the result of other forces than those engendered by the schools. It was based in part upon an assumed universality of religious belief, so widely taken for granted that one need hardly be surprised that attacks on dissenters were as vigorous and outrageous as those chronicled in the history of Christian persecutions. It is instructive to note that when Julian strove to re-establish the glory of ancient Rome he did not subsidize education but tried instead to revive the pagan creed. In part also unity was the result of the remarkable efficiency of governmental agencies, which relied upon services having little or no association with education. As long as these two bases of the established order remained firm, the fringes of society were guaranteed against crumbling. But when they gave way, there was nothing upon which the ancient world could any longer stand.

I believe, as a result of weighing this evidence with such care as I have been able to expend on it (and it is evidence which a study of the Christian empire of Europe would reinforce), that we are making a grave error if we assume that education in our time can contribute much more than it did two thousand years ago toward effecting a working agreement among the minds of men. To be sure, the university has taken over the functions once exercised by the Roman army. Technology is not any longer the affair of apprenticeship but of the scientifically controlled laboratory. And it is also true that since this technology contributes to the well-being of the average man, one reason for confidence in the stability of the prevailing social order remains. The other traditional pillar of society, namely religious belief, has to a great extent ceased to be an effective support. Though there are millions of men and women in the Western world who still subscribe to the faiths which contributed to the building of the West, it is religious dissension rather than unity which characterizes the civilization of the present.

A number of measures have been suggested for giving to education the function of religion in the same way as the function of engineering (or science, if you will) has been entrusted to it. Some hold that our whole educational system should be asked to teach "the American way of life," and others have said that controlling the school systems of enemy or conquered peoples would constitute a contribution to world morals. Still others are of the opinion that our school system must itself acquire a set of spiritual objectives, though one cannot discern any marked agreement about the character of these objectives. I gather that there is little likelihood that even philosophy, were it limited to the quest of a social morality meaningful for the youth of our day, could be introduced without extreme difficulty.

For my part, I think that we shall have to accept education as a process limited in efficiency by tendencies implicit in its very nature. It is quite unimpeachable so long as it is concerned with quantities, as was antique engineering. Sulphuric acid simply will not be another kind of acid, regardless of what students and teachers say. But as soon as there is discussion of the qualitative, or value, aspects of life, the scene will be dominated by the kind of logic and the amount of adjudicating experience which the participants possess. Here, no doubt, a rather simple rule of thumb applies. The more highly specialized a teacher is, the smaller the area of his experience with the manifold aspects of life will probably be; and the more emotional the student is, the less probable it becomes that his logic will be above suspicion. Nevertheless, if matters proceed as they have been proceeding, the chances are that on the one hand specialization will be still more sought after, while emotionalism will be intensified by the pressure of the over-all cultural agencies of the modern world— the radio, the motion picture, and the forum. To illustrate: Every year so many thousands of books are issued by American publishers alone that a worker in a given field of inquiry can hope to read only a few of them and will as a consequence be compelled to select those which deal with subjects relatively familiar to him. Similarly it is difficult to believe that the American child, asked daily to make up his mind in a hurry about complex and vital issues by adults whose success is dependent upon ability to evoke surprise and partisanship, will learn the art of noncommittal caution.

I think that at this point we might well go back to Cicero and say that the pursuit of wisdom is not to be carried on through scholarship alone. For the delving intellectual worker must always determine how matters really stood. He is a sort of burglar seeking to decipher the combinations to the safes of the past. Assuredly he must be the most objective of mortals, who cannot dispense with impartiality even for the sake of a flash of insight. It has often been said that the weakness of scholarship is in its inability to exercise the critical faculty, for criticism in the real sense is observation, co-experience, and evaluation. Yet still more obvious is the inability of the scholar to spare time in order to release the creative faculty in himself. Should he do so he would be concerned with his own brain children and not with those of others—he would be engaged in search rather than in research. To say these things is not to belittle scholarship. For what should we do without it? But we do need to remember that criticism and creation are the progenitors of wisdom. Age need wither neither of them, though it may well alter rapture into reflection.

The real difficulty about growing older is that so many of us are not malleable. It was wittily said of Charles Beard that he went from Hegel to Marx, and from Marx to Hegel. But at least he went, if not very far. The noblest report we have about St. Thomas is that when the *Summa* had been completed, he journeyed on to sanctity. Concerning another and lesser philosopher, Schelling, many have said that he taught several kinds of doctrine with the passing of the years. Perhaps the divagations were a little bizarre. And yet? He managed not to be a person who said the same things at seventy that he did when he was nineteen. A student of modern literature can encounter no more stimulating mind than that of Newman secure in the possession of ripe wisdom. Nor is he likely to find a more absorbing book than *Faust*.

I think that the college and the university of the future will be a place in which the limitations of education in the strict sense are recognized. Everybody will understand that in the business of associating youth with age so that both may learn together one must reckon with the inexperience of the young man and the too narrowly channeled learning of the old. The college graduate will still have a great many unanswered questions in his notebook, and the Ph.D. will concede that familiarity with the subjunctive in Apollonius Rhodius would inspire no Sophoclean drama. If, however, both could know that the later years of notable men had been set aside for the pursuit of wisdom, what a difference it would make! We may as well dream of a new world in which anyone who desists after his fiftieth year from gainful employment, in order to devote time and energy to the task of thinking through his experience for the benefit of himself and his fellows, will be exempt from all taxes.

Such men will not write a great deal. But from time to time, I trust, they may say something in which humor, caution, and learning are blended with a deep concern for everlasting values. Perhaps in that blessed era one or two of them will receive honorary degrees, even though they cannot endow the university with a chair for the study of Belgian marbles and Egyptian miniatures. It may even be that someone will be signally honored for having suggested that prayer is an intellectual exercise.

ON
CATHOLIC EDUCATION*

I MAY PERHAPS BE PARDONED FOR BEGINNING THESE REMARKS IN A reminiscent mood. More than thirty years ago there appeared in *America* an article by a brash young man, asking whether there were any Catholic scholars amongst us, and replying pretty much in the negative. That young man was I; and he still has cause to remember the slings and arrows which beset him from all sides. But what few have realized is that the essay in question was inspired by a distinguished silent collaborator—Father James Burns, then president of Notre Dame. At that time he had a secretary who happened also to be a much beloved student of mine, who subsequently became the Reverend John Cavanaugh, and who in due course was in turn the president of his alma mater. It is, one hopes, not injudicious to remark that in continuity there is strength. Yet continuity does not mean that the world stands still. The problem of effective Catholic scholarship remains, but it would certainly be erroneous to suppose that no progress has been made toward solving it during recent decades.

The remarks which follow will not be primarily another set of reflections of that theme, but will be concerned, perhaps somewhat too ambitiously, with the whole range of Catholic education in the United States and, however perfunctorily, with the social setting in which it has developed. We shall rule out as purely theoretical such questions as what would have happened if the

* Delivered on June 14, 1958, as part of a symposium on "The Catholic Contribution to American Intellectual Life," sponsored by the Thomas More Association and the Department of Library Science, Rosary College, River Forest, Illinois.

Faribault Plan, sponsored by Archbishop John Ireland, had been adopted. Certainly not a few persons, clerical and lay, still regret that it was not. But we are no more able to go back to it than we can get Lenin out of the train to Russia placed at his disposal in 1918 by General Ludendorff. What alone matters now is to see as clearly as we can how well the structure erected is functioning and then to inquire into the desirability of alterations and improvements. Something similar scholastic America is now everywhere doing, with a vigor which the judicious and their opposites are daily manifesting.

As for the manifesto which will now be offered you, a word of warning is no doubt suggested. You will not hear an acrimonious diatribe nor will a coat of gleaming whitewash be applied to the façade of Catholic education. It so happens that, except for my university training, I am the product of that education. There is no part of it, save for the first years of the elementary school when I happened to be like Huckleberry Finn, which I do not hold in affectionate and grateful memory. It is likewise true that for nearly two decades I have tried to do everything in my power to make a college conducted under public auspices realize all its potential strength. I hold it also in affectionate esteem, and rejoice particularly in the fact that not a few of its graduates have entered religious orders, or have gone into the Protestant mission field, or have become rabbis or wives of rabbis. As a result, I know that people say many things about Catholic education which are not true, and that others say other things about public education which are incorrect and unwise. We shall not be concerned with these. The business before us is to remember that some of us become teachers because a whale of a lot of the rest of us must learn. Upon what is taught and learned the future of the nation depends. There is no way in which we can divorce the well-being of the Church in the United States from the intellectual security of the country. We who are in the business of education must therefore ask ourselves probing questions. But as we do so we need not dangle before our eyes such fairy tales as that everybody in Russia knows as much at sixteen as anybody over here does at forty.

As a sort of text, let me cite some words by Emerson, spoken to the students of Dartmouth College long ago. Having alluded to the tradition of scholarship, he said:

Meanwhile I know that a very different estimate of the scholar's profession prevails in this country, and the importunity with which society presses its claim upon young men tends to pervert the views of youth in respect to the culture of the intellect. Hence the historical failure on which Europe and America have so freely commented. This country has not fulfilled the reasonable expectation of mankind.

Since that time, to be sure, the university has come of age in our land and there is no dearth of scholarly activity. The present era is, however, reshaping Emerson's comment in terms of education. Are our schools wasting human resources? Have they set their goals sufficiently high? Above all, has the social "importunity" of which Emerson spoke led us astray?

Now I believe we may say quite earnestly that a wholly different kind of drive and drift have been evident among American Catholics. Certainly there has been a bourgeoning which one cannot look upon without a kind of awe and a sense that a benediction has been upon us. Whose breath is not taken away when at Holy Day noontime in any great city there stream into the streets countless thousands whose goal is the Mass, to be shared in with reverent joy; or when on Ash Wednesdays there appears on the foreheads of stenographers and salesmen, teachers and students, the smudge of mortality; or when having entered into holy wedlock, thought of self is left behind by the girl who hitherto seemed to have no concern save lipstick or a hair-do, and the child is reared by her to that role in the Kingdom of Heaven which was the Saviour's supreme assignment? Out of industrial housing developments, from behind stockyards, not far from pigsties and clearings in the forest most of us have come, not very long ago. But there was a chrism on our poverty and we kept it as an heirloom, not always comprehending what glory was hidden in it, seldom perhaps associating it at all with the intelligence, yet somehow holding it upon our hearts as that which would deflect the bullets of an alien time.

We too had our revolt of the masses in the age of machines. The great growing strength of the labor unions carried most of us up the ladder of the living wage. We could now flex our muscles on picnic grounds, could siphon off the payroll dollars with which to build schools next to churches. The nation became a "social democracy" and what this change has meant to the sociology of Catholics in America staggers the imagination. For with the trend away from farms to industrial centers their initial disadvantage of being workers in textile mills and steel foundries, as compared with the settled older rural population, was overcome almost in the twinkling of the eye of history. Sons and daughters went off to college in ever increasing numbers. The O'Malleys of Salem moved out of a cold-water flat into a Cadillac. The Schulzes of Milwaukee went from the cobbler's last to the management of industry. As for most other folks, the principal grouses became death and taxes. Death helped to keep them close to the confessional; and taxes induced a measure of sobriety and frugality. At any rate, the balance sheet indicates that the American Catholic was groomed for the pursuit of happiness. This would not seldom inundate him, tear him from his moorings, make him more of a Gradgrind and less of a reformed Scrooge, and lead his pastors, anxious about youth, to liken the neighborhood movie house to Gomorrah. But by and large, the lifeline to eternity did not break.

One big reason why it did not break is the Teaching Sister. Another is the Teaching Brother, whose lack of prominence in the discussion which follows is the result of purely rhetorical considerations. Without the generations of nuns who have worked and are working in them, the parochial schools would have remained occasional little academic experiment stations. Let me repeat here what I have said before: This sacrifice of noble and devoted women to the cause of education is no doubt as glorious and moving as anything in the history of the Church in the United States, but it is also from many points of view very costly, indeed. It has with implacable permanence fed into the unending, burdensome process of elementary education, a large number of the morally and intellectually gifted. More than that, whenever there have not been enough Sisters the solution of the problem has been to add steadily to the load carried by them as individuals. Why should one not occasionally reckon with this side of the ledger when educational assets are being considered? Behind the statistics wait flesh and blood and spirit, and these are very precious things.

It is of course true that nobody can understand parochial school education who fails to see that willfully missing Mass on Sunday is far more dire according to the standards of that education than failure to know that two and two are four. And so critics who view the Sister with acrimonious dislike hold that she is shockingly underpaid, priest-ridden, wholly deprived of freedom of thought and expression, carefully insulated from the ways of the world. Contempt for the Catholic school and the women who teach in it is more widespread and bitter than most of us realize. And it is rooted, if Blanshardian fears of Catholic power are left aside, in the inability of a semi-secularist time to understand the stern sweetness of religious discipline; and this opacity in turn has its source in the loss of intimate, concrete conviction that the world is in its innermost core Divinely Personal rather than scientifically impersonal. But who does not wonder upon occasion if Catholics for their part also fail to comprehend? Does not the matter for very many stand so that the child is believed to be safer with the nuns than elsewhere, or that sending it to a parochial school is an act of obedience, often at best reluctant, comparable to putting an envelope into the collection basket or making one's Easter duty? Nor is this perfunctory collaboration, viewed now and then as a tyrannical imposition, greatly altered by coating it with sentimental varnish—by conjuring up blond curls shorn in the days of a Sister's youth, by counting on the value of her prayers in the quest of such commodities as jobs and husbands, or repeating the nonsense that nuns fret not in their narrow rooms.

The true source of a Sister's strength and the very heart of the reward which makes her spirit bloom and flower is the community to which she belongs. This appears to be veiled from our sight. It is singular that whereas the principal forms of the religious life of men—Jesuit, Benedictine, Dominican, for example —emerge as distinct and in some ways even divergent, the communities of nuns appear to be linked in an array which would be uniform were it not for the outward symbol of the habit. Even the best books about them individually seem to tell pretty much the same story, save when the personality of a Foundress or Superior is etched in recognizable contours. Yet anyone who has worked closely with Sisters knows that one community will be radically different in spirit and quality from another. The *Englische Fraeulein* of Austria, for example, are as distinct from the Madames of the Sacred Heart as Boston is from Tyler, Texas. To meet with a community which is presided over by a woman of great qualities reared in the spirit of a noble rule, is to be in a company no salon could rival. But to sit with one held together by nothing save the vows its members have taken is to have another experience entirely.

Therefore the absence of a typology seems highly regrettable. For any essay in constructive criticism of the Catholic educational effort in the lower schools would have to begin with that. Some communities have produced a long line of excellent teachers who have carried on first-rate instruction. Others have manifestly done less well. A given band of Sisters can weather the hurly-burly of urban living with a blend of gusto and serenity. Others thrive only in rural surroundings. Surely one is entitled to say in explanation that in many instances there has been a fortunate combination of rule, tradition, resources and leadership, resulting in service to American education which is beyond all price, but that this has by no means always been the case. Would it not therefore be wise to discern where excellence lies and channel the idealism of young women accordingly? Does it not sometimes seem that the quest for a quantitative attainment of the educational goal appears to involve forgetting that not every Sister everywhere can be placed in a classroom with confidence? I think that among competent educators, regardless of how far removed from the Catholic Church they are, there would be no doubt whatever that many Sisters are among the best teachers the nation knows. They do not like to see them burdened to near the margin of no return. Nor do we relish seeing them lumped with others whom neither aptitude nor training has adequately equipped for the task. Nothing could be further from my mind than to become embroiled in ecclesiastical controversy. But is it not obvious that the maxim "every child in a Catholic school" can be a perilous slogan if only because the Papal Encyclical to which all of us hark back in the discussion of educational matters, that of the great Pope Pius XI, specifically stipulates that the quality of instruction must be of the most admirable texture?

But the major point is that fruitful, mutually satisfactory cooperation between teaching Sisters and Catholic parents, now regrettably more infrequently achieved than is desirable, will come about far less as a result of establishing PTA's and similar organizations, however valuable these may be, than of informed awareness of the goals which a given community of nuns has set for itself, of its history, and of the steps it has sacrificially taken to qualify its members for their tasks. We should know, as parents, that behind every Ursuline nun there stands not only St. Angela herself but also a mighty river into which the rills of many generations have poured their waters. I do not see how, under conditions which now exist, any such knowledge can come to the average parishioner. Does he hear a reference to it from the pulpit? And certainly, were he to turn to the journals which are edited for parochial schoolteachers, he would find the same pedagogical twaddle which is served by comparable secular periodicals, however heavily sprinkled it might be with holy water.

Admittedly one cannot avoid knowing that teaching has been an anonymous profession in the United States. Public school superintendents are of course in the limelight as beleaguered and sometimes valiant whipping boys for boards of education. But teachers? Miss Daly, having said good-by to her charges of the fifth grade, sinks into community oblivion as if the ground had swallowed her. Who is told about the deeply religious men and women in the public schools who bring a profound sense of spiritual dedication to their tasks? Who save a few priests of insight and generosity ever remembers them in prayer? Who during the recent almost puerile clamor stopped to think that the situation could not be as dire as it was described with them in the picture? This is the fate of the Teaching Sister, too, and of course we all clearly realize that there must be cloisters in the religious life. But why think always about the dangers of public relations and never of the opportunities? True enough, demons lurk to assail the souls of religious, yet surely the Lord is also their ally. How good it is for the rest of us, and I trust for her also, when the Sister can emerge from seclusion and join in some collective educational enterprise! I cherish the memory of a dinner of Milton experts which heard a charming and learned nun say that she prayed daily to St. John Milton. This remark quite bowled over some of the nation's most erudite professors. There may have been a bit of cloistral simplicity in it, to be sure, but also great insight and glorious charity. We need both.

For such reasons the value of a good college to any community is very great, dubious though one may be whether all those now established will continue for long to be viable enterprises. The college gives institutional expression to the community's religious and educational ideals; affords opportunity for scholarship and creative writing; and provides a sort of hearth fire round which the hard-pressed and heavily burdened can rally. No one can fail to see that the garnered intellectual fruits are many. Already it is true that, exception having been made for the Society of Jesus, the Sisters of college faculties are making the most notable contributions to scholarship directly fostered by Catholic academic institutions, as well as to creative writing. As one might expect, most of the scholarship is in the field of what we call the humanities—

Newman in his time more sensibly used the word literature. And of course, while Americans generally pay lip service to these branches of learning, they have a Hooper rating far below that of either atomic physics or televised comic opera. One can only hope that the major communities of Sisters can keep their colleges going. The trend is against them, primarily it may be because of the lure of coeducation, which might, however, be offset by a well-considered policy of affiliation with nearby colleges for men. There are other adverse factors: the income tax bill, which forces parents against the wall of no economic return; student week ends at home, facilitated by easy transportation; the need for diversified vocational inlays; the imprint left on all youth by the mass media. The situation is therefore not an easy one. For my part, I do not see how our communities of Sisters can maintain the quality of the service they give unless their colleges do survive and prosper. For those I know somewhat, I entertain the deepest respect.

It is all very well to throw an aura of nobility round the Teaching Sister by referring to the reward which awaits her in heaven for having, as a result of the treadmill she often works in, worn the equivalent of stigmata here below. But let us listen carefully to the words of John Henry Cardinal Newman, who assuredly cherished the ascetic life: "Knowledge is one thing, virtue another; good sense is not conscience, refinement is not humility, nor is largeness and justice of view faith." It will forever remain the proper function of education to insure that as large a number of young people as possible will have knowledge, refinement, and largeness of view. How can a teacher inculcate these in others unless she have time and opportunity to acquire them for herself? We should husband our Teaching Sisters as if they were the most priceless of seedlings and ask them to expend themselves only for purposes consonant with the best aspirations of the academic calling.

Little will be said here about the parochial high school. For whatever may be averred in favor of such institutions from the point of view of the moralist and the teacher of religion, the plain fact is that the basic educational problems posed by such schools are not solved under Catholic auspices any more than they are under public ones. When one discovers (as I have) that seniors of a high school bearing proudly its dedication to Aquinas do not have the foggiest notion who he may have been, the prognosis is not less bleak than it is when one finds out that the seniors of Thomas Jefferson High School do not realize that he wrote the Declaration of Independence. The country generally has suffered intellectually from a failure to sense that the age of puberty is not merely the age of puberty. I shall permit myself the dubious luxury of just one further comment. If the reason for assuming the onerous burden of the Catholic high school is primarily pastoral, then possibly one should determine how the best results can be obtained from the effort expended. Now the situation may well be that in good academic public high schools, where the standards are reasonably rigorous and well-established Newman Clubs are in existence, young people suffer no impairment of their faith. Indeed there are such institutions which can even point to a higher incidence of religious vocations among their graduates than that found in Catholic high schools. The situation is different in establishments in urban areas which must admit all and sundry. There the risk of moral infection is serious, indeed, and one must also gravely fear that religious faith and practice will become steadily more tenuous. But is it not the truth that the Catholic high school musters in young people who would in all likelihood fend very well for themselves, and turns over to the public authorities those most in need of religious solicitude?

Here is a problem not easily solved and which is bound to become more perplexing as the era of the great internal migration goes on. As never before the nation is on the move, now not because great immigrant masses seek homes and jobs, but because the shift to the cities of hitherto underprivileged rural populations coincides with the relocation of industry on a prodigious scale. This means not merely the uprooting of old ties for which no substitutes can readily be found, but social conflict as well, with inevitable effects on morals and morale. The demands on edu-

cation are already heavy and will become increasingly more difficult to meet. In particular guidance and counseling services must
be provided, the number of retarded children for whom urban
schools will be asked to care will surely increase, and certain
groups of maladjusted teen-agers will be more in evidence than
they are even at present.

This is neither the time nor the place for a probing discussion
of finance, which is as inseparable from education as buying shoes
for children is from matrimony. But if Catholic education is to
do its share of the work imposed on us by all the great migration
now in progress, help must come to it from somewhere. A large
number of the parents involved will be able to make little if any
contribution to the maintenance of schools for a long time to
come. I should think that even a society like ours, which builds
a high fence between Church and state (a fence incidentally, it
is well to remember, which has often provided Catholics with
better neighbors than they would otherwise have had), might
well come to realize that the situation with which it is having
and will have to cope is one in which religious motivation can
be of the greatest social value, and that therefore the community
as a whole ought not to deal in a niggardly fashion with the
social welfare aspects of religious education conducted under
whatever auspices. But having said this, we should quickly add
that it will be as out of key to be optimistic on this score as a
song from *Oklahoma* would be at a funeral.

At this point one who has no special competence in the teaching of religion but who has had occasion over not a few decades
to evaluate some of its fruits may, perhaps, be allowed to make
a few comments on one or the other of its aspects. There can
be no doubt that in this area children profit by some of the
oldest uses of project methods. The boy acolyte comes breath-
takingly close to the Mass; the little girl who strews flowers on
Holy Thursday identifies herself with service to her Lord; children bless themselves with holy water, St. Francis gave them the
Christmas crib, they live in a world of bowed heads, folding
hands, genuflections, burning candles. The way to the reality of

First Holy Communion thus passes through a field of symbols every flower in which is precious. No one who has walked there can forget—not Renan or James Joyce or Mary McCarthy.

But the times come when questions are asked. These will at first be the interrogation points of innocent rebellion. But later on they will harden into negations. The world of concrete symbol will change into one of intellectual abstractions and emotional fixations. In this last there will loom up as large as the moon the question as to the relationship between freedom and obedience. This is the most fateful of the warning signals that maturity is impending. One can only be candid and admit that the more of ripeness there is, the greater the danger to the religious spirit. There could be no point in denying that Newman wrote the *Grammar of Assent,* and that indeed it was imperative he do so. In the face of a perennial peril he offered, anxiously and painstakingly, a path to salvation. That path is not paved with the symbols we have noted with grateful reverence. It is hewn through the rock of intellectual doubt with the pickaxe of analysis.

It is, in my judgment, during the years identified with the high school that everything will depend, at least for the most gifted and the more turbulent, upon how ably and deftly the young person is led from the land of obedience to the symbol to that other of the freedom to question and to weigh answers. Of course one can go on for a long time saying and doing hallowed things without any longer believing in them. But normally the boy or girl of nineteen will have chosen, often quite unconsciously, to be or not to be in the spiritual sense. How grave the responsibility therefore is! How easily an unwise curb or an injudicious answer can bring a soul to a road which may for some distance seem parallel but which in actuality is veering off! One can only hope that those whom education so heavily burdens will have the strength and the wisdom required. Even when the best is done there will be strange, inexplicable failures. When it is not done, God help us! Men like me have comparable experiences in the teaching of English, writing, history, but these do not mean the same thing in terms of life. Should we ever forget that it is the dangerous glory of Catholic education to place in the foreground considerations which if they had never been placed there might not loom so large and challenging? Who could venture to offer advice here? One can only pray, hope, and indeed suffer with those upon whom the burden is laid. At least we should all know that it is being borne and not expect that miracles will be wrought either by sentimentalism or by smart new approximations to a theology for mass consumption.

We come therewith to higher education concerning which, to paraphrase Montaigne, all the needful things have long since been said. It remains for us to put some of them into actual practice. First, there is the vexing business about Catholic scholarship. Obviously there are three seed beds in which such scholarship could grow: the religious orders, the priesthood, and the laity. We can with some assurance say of the first that in accordance with their several traditions they will and have already begun to carry on studies of depth and pertinence in the field of religion. The Jesuits of Woodstock, the Benedictines of Collegeville, fruitfully husbanding the rich legacy of Virgil Michel, the Franciscan Conference—these are estimable achievements by any intellectual standard and one may thank God for them. But it would be unrealistic to assume that the orders can make a very significant contribution to the vast enterprise of secular scholarship. The fact is that in the first instance young people who join them seldom have at the core of their reflection becoming eminent in research. Crashaw said of St. Teresa that she was for the Moors and martyrdom. So it will always be with those who resemble her and it is good so.

The priesthood makes evident the sacrifice which is the other side of one of the special glories of the Church. Many generations of American intellectuals and leaders in all fields of inquiry have a background of family life associated with the rabbinate or the ministry. Indeed, it is probably not too much to say that without the love of learning which has been zealously inculcated in such households, the history of leading American academic institutions would be far less illustrious than is the case. Of necessity such a tradition cannot be fostered among Catholics, which is not an argument against celibacy, dictated as that is by far more transcendent considerations. But there can be no human gain without a compensatory sacrifice. Some secular priests will be first-rate historians, musicologists, sociologists. These will loom up as exceptions to the prevailing rule.

The only way, then, that a tradition of Catholic scholarship—or rather, perhaps, of Catholic participation in scholarly activities—can be firmly established is to use lay men and women as the foundation. This is rather obvious, but when one asks how this is to be done people begin to talk about the weather. We shall venture to refer to other matters. It is the university which constitutes the scholar's smithy. The quality of the work done in it will depend upon the quality of the master smiths and on how well their skill and industry are communicated to apprentices. The college for its part will thrive as its associations with the university do. It so happens that I preside over an institution the scholarly achievements of whose faculty are in several ways quite remarkable. There is no doubt in my mind that this has to a great extent been made possible by the continuing vital relationships between this group and the illustrious universities of the area in which we work. And I am reminded also that in times past it was the tie of mutual respect and admiration which existed between English scholars in the college which is today according us hospitality and the University of Chicago which made for a remarkable flowering of learning here.

If, then, there were a Catholic university in which Catholic lay men and women could live and work on a level of equality with the best scholars in the most reputable non-Catholic institutions, and if such a university had grown to maturity during a hundred years, I am sure the many colleges which have struggled into being under the auspices of religious orders would have a lifeline to a center of intellectual activity which would immensely hearten and strengthen them. We have as yet no such university, and unless there is a change in the way things are going we never will have one. Far too many so-called universities have reared their heads, and we may as well be honest and admit that in none of them do lay men and women have the status, the freedom, or the function of co-building which would as a matter of course be theirs at any distinguished secular center of studies. To some extent the problem is one of relatively meager salaries, but this may well be not the most important thing at all. There are state universities which keep good faculties together despite wage scales below the norm. There are private secular colleges which do likewise. But it is wholly impossible to create a fraternity of scholars unless one first kindles the spark of cooperation. And so we should at long last ask ourselves some really incisive questions, painful and embarrassing though they may be. To what extent is a Catholic university ready to accord to those it has chosen to be its professors full equality of status, whether they be religious or lay folk? Will it give the professor an opportunity to help shape the policies, of all kinds, which are to govern the institution as a whole? Will he be consulted, for example, when a new president is chosen, or when new members of the faculty are to be recruited?

Until such questions (and there are other cognate ones) can be answered affirmatively there can come into being no tradition of Catholic scholarship which rests on a continuing progression of lay men and women through the generations. As things are at present, nothing akin to the solidarity of working Catholic scholars is indicated. Not a few of the best among those who serve Catholic education, clerical and lay, have their closest personal and intellectual ties with the secular universities in which they came to know the meaning and the value of graduate study. I am far from certain that this may be anything less than highly desirable. Anyone who reads the published correspondence of the eminent Jesuit paleontologist, Père de Chardin, will wonder less whether his best work could have been done unless he had been linked with science as a whole, studied under Catholic auspices or not, than whether his quite unusually significant contributions to religious literature would have had their remarkable pertinence and influence unless he had moved with assurance and freedom on the ground of science in his time.

Of one thing I am at any rate certain after many years of association with academic life. The attempt to evaluate higher education from the pastoral point of view is always bound to come round to endorsing what Newman said a hundred years ago. Knowledge will not make people better, just as ignorance will not make them more educated. The sovereign justification of a Catholic university, he held, is that it can and ought to have a school of theology. To be sure such schools have been established at secular universities in Germany, but we are not likely to do anything of the kind in the United States. Newman reasoned thus: "You will break into fragments the whole circle of secular knowledge if you begin with the mutilation of the divine." That remark is profoundly true. It is the severance of theology from the university far, far more than the public school which for a long time was responsible for the rise of secularism. A Catholic student at the University of Munich who knows that on certain days Romano Guardini, to whom the whole world listens, will be lecturing, quite automatically makes room for theology in his view of life. And one may note that the presence of Union Theological Seminary on the campus of Columbia University has altered the academic experience of countless students. May it therefore not be regrettable that only the Catholic University of America has a Catholic faculty of theology?

However one may respond to such a query, the argument that a need for broader opportunities to exercise pastoral care justifies the insistence on more and more Catholic universities will not, I think, hold much water. In the long run the only valid reason for going to a university is to obtain what a university, with its traditions, professors, laboratories, and library has to offer. To assume that because able and sagacious religious pour out their hearts' blood in the effort to keep institutions going, the holiness of their graduates or their ability to move to the forefront of the scholarly procession will be guaranteed, is to run afoul of statistics. It is to be sure true that the temper of the time makes a plea for walled towns plausible. But I often wonder whether the grumbling which goes on in such towns, with their restricted horizons and (figuratively) their antiquated plumbing, may not do more to undermine sincerity of religious conviction than does exposure to the wide and admittedly wicked world.

Let me hope that what has been said will not seem to contain a measure of captiousness or condescension. Perhaps it would help if, as one who has many years of a varied career behind him, I made a quite personal statement at this point. No man could hold the Society of Jesus in greater esteem than do I. There is no other organization of men which has exerted so profound an influence on my life, though I have never studied under its auspices. In Germany, France, and the United States the followers of St. Ignatius have sustained and directed my thought, and it would be impossible to find words in which to express adequately my gratitude to and my affection for them. If I have challenged and in some measure kept the faith, it is to their example and to the grace of God that this is largely due. Nor could anyone be unmindful of all they have done in the United States to improve the institutions of higher learning which are under their auspices. But I shall say frankly that in this matter of the multiplication of universities they are unintelligible to me. They may be right as they are in many other things, but at least I should like to enter a demurrer.

The result of this multiplication is that religious admirably trained in important areas of learning are being tied to back-breaking administrative posts. They wrestle manfully with budgets, stage fund-raising dinners (as do I), cope with faculties perennially underpaid. Meanwhile Catholic enrollments in public and other nonreligious centers of higher education increase by leaps and bounds. Father X is busily computing tuition fees paid in to a School of Law by young men who never have and never will have any interest in Catholic doctrine, while Father Y on the campus of a secular university preaches a streamlined Sunday sermon to thousands of students in a gymnasium. Would it not serve the cause of religion far better if the example of Oxford were followed, as Newman in his day advocated, and foundations were established which the society is uniquely fitted to maintain? I cannot help believing that a hundred Campion Houses serving institutions as diverse as Harvard and Pennsylvania State would not merely take care of the spiritual needs of vast numbers of young men and women destined to occupy positions of leadership, but would bring Catholic learning into a totally different relationship to American intellectual life. In short, why not give the Jesuit Mark Hopkins a log rather than a cabin?

Let me close with a brief comment on the over-all intellectual situation. It is apparent that the social future will be entrusted to the scientist and the engineer. Whether they rule dictatorially, according to an efficiency table on which human resources are listed and evaluated by bureaucratic rule of thumb, or according to patterns which permit of individualistic deviations from the norm, we shall as a race for a long time to come have a queer feeling that we are figures on a logarithmic chart. It will be difficult to gainsay that so many hours of such a kind of work will produce a desired result in terms of human happiness; and at the same time the temptation will arise to consider this result the only thing necessary. Concern with religious ends and values may well become for many quite peripheral.

At work here is a mighty force which has already in many parts of the world torn millions from their spiritual moorings. Its product is the materialism which the Church in Europe has long since identified. Therefore it may well be providential that, just when it almost came to seem that the highest good of the race might well be air conditioners for many and trips to the moon for some, a new way of appraising intellectual endeavor has suggested itself. Already adumbrated by such writers as Von Huegel and Lecomte du Nouy, it has found its most brilliant contemporary expression in the writings of Père de Chardin. Scholarly work is viewed as a form of participating in the realization of God's will, and not as tangential, of this world only, or at best apologetic in some unclear way. It remains as always the quest for truth, to be carried on with sincerity and zeal, but is also a

sharing, awesome and sanctifying, with Christ of His world—
a world which is coming more and more to seem not a panorama
of things fixed in space of time—not for example Mont Blanc or
the Justinian Code—but an ever-moving film of the Creator's idea.
Reality is for the imaginative scholar a dream, but not one which
fades or passes away. It is a phase of the vision which has been
held in the Divine Mind eternally. Seeing the structure of the
molecule we are at His side. And being there must of necessity
be good. If this be so man moving from the shadows of things
into their essences at the scholar's behest will gain that awareness
of the spirit which no being immured in the illusory material can
any longer dispel. At least we may hope that it will be so.

CENTENNIAL ADDRESS*

IN THE ONCE BEAUTIFUL OLD CITY OF HILDESHEIM THEY WERE wont to show, in the cathedral close, a rose tree which had grown there during a thousand years; and one could not help thinking then of the generations of children who had come each spring to observe in it the ever-repeated miracle of light and flower. So it is with a seat of learning. To have taught young people here, summer and winter and spring, during a hundred years is to have well earned the right to look back and forward, to recall a dream, and to speculate on its ultimate fruition. It is a great honor for me to come here as a stranger and try to put something of what you must sense into a very few words.

No doubt the only reason why I should feel at all confident of my ability to embark on this adventure is that I have long since entertained a deep personal affection for the religious community to which this university, like many another school, owes its existence. How great a wonder of the spirit it seems in retrospect that after the French Revolution, which had tried to root out of the soil of France every vestige of the Christian faith, there should have sprung up from it so many blessed groups of men and women resolved not merely to profess anew at home what had been proscribed—cross and Mass, creed and sanctity— but also to carry the same profession round the wide world with a kind of holy and humble imperialism. To these communities the Middle West of our country in particular owes more than it can ever repay for precept, example, and dedication. And I sup-

* Reprinted from the University of Dayton *Exponent,* issue of April 1950, pp. 3–5, 22. The address was delivered at the centennial convocation of the university.

pose that the priest who a century ago came from Alsace to the then little town of Dayton and set to work trying to change what had been a farm into a struggling school must in some eternal leisure hours think gratefully that the Lord has multiplied the seed he sowed far beyond any vision of harvest he had entertained.

Today we have come to a sort of question mark in education which would have seemed to the founder of your university very strange indeed. For him the pattern of learning was relatively simple and steadfast. The school was to concern itself with the blending of the medieval curriculum—*trivium* and *quadrivium*—with the humanistic classicism which had been one of the great intellectual achievements of the Renaissance. For Catholic schools the pattern had been very skillfully devised by the followers of St. Ignatius during two centuries of enthusiastic and creative teaching. It was meant to produce men for whom the central tradition of thought, letters, and art would remain a treasure less sacred and fructifying only than their religion. You put St. Paul, Plato, and Vergil into your intellectual knapsack and went out to meet the world.

In our time, this concept of the educated life has become one which only a few Americans would not consider outmoded and rather queer if it were presented to them. By dint of adapting the college and the university to the dynamic forces operating in our society we have wedded education to political, economic, and technical action to an extent unparalleled in other countries, though of course something of the sort has been happening there, too. Our students want, when their campus days are over, to get aboard the moving train of their time—the ceaselessly throbbing chariot of industry, technological advancement, and government. It is not so much that they are scornful of everything not manifestly utilitarian as that they are fearful lest their concern with such matters might handicap them in the inevitable race. And in all truth this race has become a pretty strenuous and exciting affair. A hundred years ago, for example, no student of medicine had, I think, even dreamed of biochemistry or of the relations between theoretical physics and therapy. Nor did there exist anything like pedagogy in our contemporary sense. Even the historical scholar, of whom I am after ten years of presidential oratory still a faint shadow, must perforce confess not merely that there is a great deal more history than there used to be but that the methods of historical study have grown incomparably more complex and exacting.

All this has gone hand in hand with startling social change. Forty years ago, the United States was still a provincial country. It is difficult to realize now that rural districts and country towns, which most of us then inhabited, were visited regularly by German peddlers, selling needles, thread, scissors and comparable articles manufactured in their country. The British pound and the French franc were a good deal steadier than the dollar. When I graduated from college, the foremost professor of psychology in the United States was Hugo Muensterberg, a German, while the most widely respected student of literature amongst us was probably the French ambassador, M. Jusserand. Within the short span of time which has elapsed, we as a people have been catapulted into the driver's seat of Western civilization. Even if one were to disregard the natural sciences and technology, the amazing advance made in the United States in such fields as political and social science and history would be breath-taking indeed.

But being at the helm has turned out to be the most challenging and dangerous enterprise in which the nation has ever engaged. The world stage has become something agonizingly like a John Wayne movie. Here we are with our fingers on a gun which can shoot A-bombs and H-bombs. Over there is Stalin similarly equipped: and the question seems to be, could we beat him to the draw? It is not so certain that we could, but even if we did the resulting desolation of the earth would be beyond remedying in any period of time we can foresee.

Were we sure that the murderous weapons of which we speak could be locked up by mutual consent, we should still have no way of telling whether fifty years hence we are likely to have succumbed to a more subtle, because ideological, attack. For the plain truth of the matter is that despite all lip service to a democratic ideal, the forms of living which have characterized the Western world have become very vague concepts for millions of men and women. Have there not been so many failures, so many betrayals, so much indifference? And have not far too many of us ceased to practice the art of thinking?

That is why a big question mark has now been affixed to the word "education." We cannot tell whether men will prove to be good and intelligent enough to use power not selfishly but democratically and for the true benefit of the race. And the reason why we can't is because we have no dependable recipe for making them be good and intelligent. What we do have is education, and this quite obviously does not do so.

To say this is not to make still another scathing attack on our colleges and universities. It is merely to suggest that either we are expecting too much of education as currently defined, or that we must try to transform it into something it has never previously been. Personally, I believe that the first statement is correct—that too much is being expected, and for the wrong reasons. The modern university can do some highly important things very well and it can in a measure provide assurance that those who study what it is doing will be competent practitioners when they leave the campus. Let me illustrate. Our system of higher learning as a whole can train a sufficiently large and able group of biologists to see to it, first, that what has hitherto been learned about biological processes and forms will not be forgotten, and second, that a fairly impressive number of new facts will be unearthed in order to enable science to correct some of the views hitherto erroneously held. In addition, the sum total of biological knowledge can be used for good and evil ends. The physician can apply it to the cure of disease. The soldier can utilize it in the dread art of biological warfare. But how it is to be used the biologist cannot determine, any more than he can tell us, as a philosopher perhaps could, why the whole realm of biological phenomena exists.

Or suppose we turn to the realm of literature, and note for example that scholarship can collect every available shred of material about the life, language, and intellectual background of Geoffrey Chaucer. It can pretty well determine how the *Canterbury Tales* sounded when the poet himself spoke the lines, and it can almost tell you, if you are interested, what books he read before he sat down to write. These are matters of great interest and importance. But not all Chaucerian scholars round the wide world could produce *The Knight's Tale* or anything comparably good. In other words, they are powerless to create a great poet, and obviously the most significant fact about Chaucer is that somehow or other he came into being.

Yes, if one ascends to the highest realm of scholarly inquiry and asks what goes on in schools of theology, one will find out that the sacred science is carefully and reverently taught to groups of interested students. There also exists a speculative theology, which seeks to derive still further salutary truth from revealed dogma. But not all the theological schools acting in unison can insure the coming of a single saint. Naturally, there may be one somewhere on the campus. Yet saints obviously keep on bobbing up in the queerest places, nowadays as always. Who would have thought that the son of a storekeeper in Assisi would become the most beloved of holy men? And who would have surmised that a little girl in the Pyrenees held in her heart the mystery of Lourdes? God seems to walk among His people and put His hand down here and yonder and say, "Come, My beloved," with no regard whatever for college or university degrees. Does He not even appear to take singular delight in finding them where a professor would never dream of looking?

This is the way human life and human history are. The great procession of the race is led by its philosophers, its poets, its statesmen, and its saints, for good or evil. We cannot manufacture them. They grow in plots by themselves in God's garden, to which as in the beginning Satan has access. All the rest of us can do is try very hard to distinguish the authentic from the sham claimants to authenticity, and tell good from evil. Were all men able to do this—only this—our world would be troubled by no such nightmares as now besiege the innermost chambers of its heart. Then should it not be the central purpose of education to increase the number of those who can distinguish?

I think most university men would agree and say: Yes, of course. But at this point they are square up against a most perplexing conundrum. Viewed in one light, the university faculty is a force of detectives finding out more and more things about the world. Keeping up with his assignment to just one case is often more than the individual scholar can accomplish. Even inquiries which have gone on for centuries—for instance, into the meaning of *Hamlet*—can never be adjudged finished because something new is constantly being learned. And so the sum total of the dossiers is so vastly much more extensive than the criminal files of the Department of Justice that one can only look on it with absolute bewilderment and nostalgic dismay.

Max Ascoli recently said something about the American newspaper which is pertinent here. He remarked that the coverage of news is now so extensive that the citizen could only stare at the huge mélange of incidents as he might at a dug-up ant heap. How can he piece together any kind of real impression of what is really happening in the world? Naturally, it is safe to say he doesn't. He has become so inured to piles of facts, that he is totally unable to distinguish a given fact from fiction. The historian is often startled by the popularity of books which profess to be well documented, but which are, if one examines the documentation with care, the work of gross and prejudiced amateurs. Under these conditions it is almost impossible for the modern mind to exercise the critical faculty which I have termed the all-important realistic business of education. We all know that just because we hear more and more about the Russians, the Germans, or the British, for example, is no reason whatever for supposing that we actually understand any of them better than we formerly did. In fact, a great deal we hear is simply rubbish.

Accordingly, educators have begun to look back with envy to the system of medieval-humantistic education which still flourished in a measure when this university was founded. Could we not peer about the library and put together those volumes which because they are the best yet written would enable the student to form dependable standards of conduct and criticism? It is, we shall confess, a very difficult assignment. The great advantage of the old culture was that only the very best books had survived. You read Homer, the Greek dramatists, Plato, Aristotle, Vergil, Cicero, Horace, and a few other writers. The rest was lost or forgotten. The Judeao-Christian tradition, for its part, was based simply on two testaments. An educational system the purpose of which was to understand these books thoroughly—that is to know their language, their content, and their form—was a system which envisaged a limited objective that could be reached.

Things are far from being that simple for us of the present. Unless one is somehow predisposed to thinking that a book is either significant or interesting in terms of one's own life, nothing is likely to make one sit up nights with it; and unfortunately people agree about neither utility nor excitement, though they are likely to subscribe to the dictum that what are ancestors called discipline is merely unreasonable torture. There is also another point to make. So aware have scientists become of their ability to take the engine of the world apart that they have grown almost feverishly anxious lest somebody be given a driver's license who does not live by a high moral code. Can we extract such a code from what is termed a program in the reading of great books? It seems to me that Cardinal Newman gave the answer many years ago. Such a program can train a generation of gentlemen—and, of course, ladies—and that is assuredly not to be underestimated. But though literature and art are of priceless value, they will regenerate no one in whom the forces of regeneration are not already at work.

The university can only assume that such forces are present. It cannot produce them. Though it is the noblest intellectual creation of man, it is neither God nor nature. And so I have long since come to the conclusion that the university must also pray. There must be associated with its realistic consciousness of its own worth the humility of insight into the fact that the order of reason it seeks to establish upon the earth will depend for its realization upon how much goodness is divinely infused into the evil which is native to man—the evil which in our times towers so huge and monstrous as to frighten all. The university can only ask fervently that there may be not only a new birth of freedom but also a resurrection of virtue.

That is why it can be an inestimable advantage for a university to have a religious orientation. For when religion is properly understood it is freedom and it is virtue. I believe indeed that it is dynamite with a soul. But does one have to say now that a faith which is merely a convention or a feeling is worse than none? Both Hitler and Stalin were trained in religious schools. The recurrence in the writings and speeches of both of phrases derived from the liturgy and the catechism reminds one of the horrible truth that the corruption of the best is the worst of all catastrophes which can beset the human race.

A great and true faith is uniquely aware of reason and mystery alike. On the one hand it cherishes reason, which is the true glory of the university—reason which may be speculative, or practical, humanistic as well as scientific, philosophical or religious in its orientation. It is man finding out, judging, comparing, planning. Yet there are vast realms of being which reason cannot explore. The human spirit is able to reach down and touch the floor of the universe, but it must take the cellar for granted. It can likewise place its hand on the ceiling of human destiny and therewith know that God exists, but it is unable to fathom the hidden things which rest in the Divine Counsel. To fancy that reason is all of man's strength is just as limiting as is the denial of reason's existence. The other day an eminent mathematician deplored the fact that so many of us tend to assume that formulas are everything and to forget that underneath them lie the atoms for which we cannot account but which we must perforce take for granted. And in quite the same way the life we live is not to be enjoyed or endured unless we are content to let it rest on pillars we cannot ourselves build, however much we may be able to erect upon them.

It is ominous and tragic alike that so many of our contemporaries have lost reason or faith or both. The great German historian, Friedrich Meinecke, commenting recently on the trends which brought his country so low, changing its beautiful cities into ribbons of ruin, said that in his opinion one of them had been the tendency to be content with a form of education designed merely to transform the student into a skilled technician. The *homo faber*, Meinecke writes, had gone out thinking that his practical job was all he needed to be trained for, only then to discover relatively late in life that there are wide and vital areas of civic and social concern. Now he hastily and credulously believed himself able to cope with these through recourse to crudely emotional and irrational devices. In all truth, may we not have put our finger here on one of the fountain sources of the totalitarian delusion, surely the most inhuman, baneful, and unreasonable of delusions? To have thought that one can add the cubits of sanctity, or poetry, or organically nurtured goodness to one's stature through some kind of random wishful thinking is, in Meinecke's opinion, the great pride which went before the fall of Germany.

It may, alas, be the great pride that goes before the downfall of our world. Therefore to kneel every morning and evening, as this your university does in a prayer of gratitude and dedication, is to supplement the goodly business of the academic day with the yearning for the rain of eternity which alone can make time flower. Of course we know that this kneeling is not enough, but that the issue will depend upon the extent to which gratitude and dedication are carried not only into life but into every hour and moment of life, and upon the individual's ability never to cease growing and inquiring even while he remains conscious of the limitations of the waxing and waning, the questioning and answering, of man.

We have no dependable defense against the assault to which civilization in our time is exposed save the strength which resides in our reasoned consciousness of why civilization is worth defending. We say to Stalin that he has thrown away the things which make life worth while—freedom and courtesy, reason and faith. Yet saying so will help little unless we have a deep, loving knowledge of them, so dynamic and contagious that it will avail even those, our brothers, who are trodden under his heel. It remains the permanent, glorious business of education to help us. Carrying on with confidence but not with pride, with integrity but not with self-esteem, with a desire for what is useful but also a yearning for what is holy, may you move forward to the end of another century in the steadfast hope that through what you do God will in some measure bless youth, our country, and all mankind.

GOOD, EVIL,
AND BEYOND*

PLATO THOUGHT THAT THE GODS WOULD NEVER DESERT A MAN DE-
termined to be just. Where for our time are the gods? And
what is justice? These are the same questions our fathers asked,
but it is harder to answer them now, for we have found out
much more about the world than our ancestors ever dreamed
of. It is important to note that the spade work has not been done
by the physical sciences only. The careful scholar has, for example, dug into every stratum of historic time and has charted
the devious courses of human thought and instinct. Whereas, to
use one illustration, no person writing five hundred years ago
in any literary language now spoken had so much as dreamed
of the Americas, though these had brought to flower at least
three rich cultures, any one of us who cares to do so may learn in
detail the customs by which Tierra del Fuegians lived three
thousand years ago.

Even the average semiliterate human being has acquired, without appreciable effort, a beguiling awareness of the world as
a whole. He is led to speak, cheerfully or in resignation, of "one
world," and to feel that the earth has obviously grown smaller.
If he is naïve, he will suppose that this sensation results from
being able to move from place to place very rapidly, by car,
airplane, or rocket. Or he may be more learned and surmise, possibly in the manner outlined by Richard Hertz in a rather notable

* Reprinted from *The Annals of the American Academy of Political and
Social Science* 249 (1947), pp. 169–176.

book,** that because no new economic areas can be found for exploitation or development, aggressive capitalism throughout the world has faded into history, taking with it uninhibited individualism. Or finally he may proceed, as a political philosopher, to declare that unless rules of social action are imposed uniformly on all peoples by all peoples, world-wide conflicts will lead to world-wide ruin. Had wars been limited, say, to conflicts between Germany and France, the atomic bomb would never have been invented. One government, we are therefore told, must speedily be devised for one world.

On the other hand, people are curiously aware that the intelligible universe has somehow grown more minutely divisible than it used to be. Manifestly the physicist has imprinted the idea of the microcosm indelibly on the mind of every citizen of this age. Or one may read of extraordinarily fruitful inquiry into the structure of organic matter, such as that recently described by Professor van Niel, and rise certain that the architect of living things is an infinitesimal fellow, indeed. But I am not thinking of smallness primarily in the scientific sense. That learning must be concerned with a vast number of little things, the dimensions of any of which we are never wholly able to determine, is a fact which at one level produces specialization, from which, alas, no efforts at synthesis will seemingly ever emancipate us. While our efforts to make one world in the intellectual sense may spur us on to select and study a hundred best books, it is clear that none of these books will mean a great deal unless there is added, by way of appendix, what generations of writers in the same field have subsequently reported. Reading Euclid is, in short, of relatively little use unless one also reads Planck.

And in another area, modern man has an uneasy feeling that any value to which he might wish to commit himself has been challenged sometime, somewhere, with arguments of such great complexity and wit that it would be futile to attempt to dispose of them. Therefore he is skeptical of all values, even those ap-

** Richard Hertz, *Man on a Rock* (Chapel Hill, N.C.: University of North Carolina Press, 1946).

plauded by the club to which he belongs, unless they are attacked by someone he dislikes. At any rate, our perception of the ever-increasing smallness of intelligible reality leads to a cynical resignation which differs from the despair of the ancient world in the significant sense that whereas that despair was rooted in a conviction that nothing could be proved true by dialectic, our resignation is born of the feeling that there is so much to know about everything that knowledge of anything specific is made impossible.

Here are the twin millstones of modern culture, and they can grind exceeding well. On the one hand we are urged to comprehend and endorse "one world"; and on the other hand we are certain that we can comprehend and endorse literally nothing. That is the central experience of our time. We know that the various energies recently released by science and already harnessed by technology are potentially more revolutionary than were coal and iron in their day. But you have only to talk with labor people a short while to realize that the common man, far from being exhilarated by the prospect, is terrified instead. He does not discern any correlation between what is being planned by the chemist and the engineer for mankind as a whole and what he, as a single little human being, dreams of for himself. That labor should now actually be engaged in organized warfare against technology is startling, in view of traditional American optimism. It means that the worker no longer believes that the inventive human mind can be trusted with human values.

Knowledge that he was caught between the millstones of the potential wealth of knowledge and the limitations of man was, for instance, what goaded on that great recorder of elemental poetic intuitions, Friedrich Nietzsche. I believe we may say that Nietzsche, an exceptionally religious man, abandoned the idea of God because he did not see how the multifarious facets of the reality made manifest in intellectual experience could be integrated. And of course the first truth about the apprehension of God is that He is integration. Being, however, a sincere and creative individualist, Nietzsche also realized that without a source of creative unity, man could have no civilization. To solve the problem, he invented the hypothesis of emerging omniscient mind. But the farther away from Nietzsche we get, the clearer it becomes that this hypothesis is untenable. It is not bettered by tinting it with fictitious Darwinism and saying that twenty-five thousand years of waiting will improve the human brain. We see only too clearly that those who propound this belief themselves deteriorate noticeably with each ten years.

Conversely, it seems to me that Karl Marx and his associates abandoned the idea of God primarily because they thought that the integration of nature and spirit, of man's vital functions and the laws of cosmic energy, was so definitive a fact that no room could be found for the individual person. And obviously the second characteristic of the idea of God is that He must be a person. But today it is quite clear that the human individual, at least, is a necessity. For he is, among other things, the leader who alone can make communism work. And more generally, the contention that economic and biological developments are so closely intertwined that they secrete the thoroughly conditioned human atom, without personality or the need for it, must surely be abandoned, for if there is anything modern history has demonstrated, it is that freedom is not a formula but a desire.

These two philosophies were inevitable products of the twin millstones; they were nobler in conception than the doctrines which were their time-born rivals, and I have no illusions about lightly disposing of them. Nevertheless, it is clear that they were attempts to substitute for the relativism of their period a fabricated absolute. If either the Marxist or the Nietzschean point of view was a satisfactory doctrine for living, why should not a blend of the two be an acceptable synthesis? Such a synthesis —and it is a formidable one—has been put forward by the totalitarians. To the Nazi, for instance, the world is nature and yet also superman. The Nazi is a socialist and yet also a thoroughly uninhibited individualist. The Stalinist differs only in color.

But now the ingredients in this mixture of philosophies suffered a tremendous change. Notable energies of a sort were released by opening the sluices in the dam. The Nazi rid himself of the social pity which is conserved in the writings of Marx, and transformed Nietzsche's superman into a ruthless and tyrannical boss. The totalitarian synthesis took away from the people their endowment of personal dignity and autonomy without offering in exchange a natural order which functioned to their advantage. A human being might well surrender some treasure of liberty for the sake of security without finding the bargain unfair. Some might even argue that all freedom could be exchanged for security, but to be robbed of liberty and still be left wholly insecure is an outrage.

I want to stress the terms freedom, security, and outrage, for if they are understood, nazism can also be in part comprehended. As late as a century ago, each of these words had two connotations for most people in the Western world. Freedom was the acquisition of a kind of social permit to act on one's own initiative, at the voting booth, let us say. But freedom also meant ability to make a personal decision about conduct and was, in short, a precious right to follow the dictates of one's own conscience. Security was a defense against need, a right to some property, but was also a state of inner equipoise resulting from the conviction that one had chosen the Good. And as for outrage, it was on the one hand an action against which the law could be invoked, and on the other hand an event which stirred the conscience to vehement and vital protest.

The totalitarian disorder is a state of mind in which the second parts of these definitions have vanished completely. The Nazi, for instance, defines liberty solely as power, security only as protection against material want, and outrage merely as misfortune through which something one has craved has been given to someone else. A master race—or, let us not forget, a self-righteous nation—is thought to have freedom only when it holds dominion over others. Security is *Lebensraum*, or an area of vassal states. Outrage is maldistribution of raw materials, prestige, or wages. In short, one-half of the domain of experience to which the three most basic human words apply no longer exists. If you have ever talked frankly with a young totalitarian, you know what it means to carry to the radical end result this restriction of reality. For him the extermination camp was not a crime but merely an efficient instrument devised by an astute collectivity for the purpose of establishing power and security. Having been trained to throw off every vestige of a commitment to older ethical views, he has become, wholly without knowing it, an emissary of hell upon the earth; for there is nothing very important to say about hell save that it is beyond good and evil.

The young totalitarian has become the sternest object lesson which modern man could have set before himself. He is far more terrible and significant than the atomic bomb. This bomb can kill—kill, perhaps, all that lives upon the earth. But the young totalitarian is not only the person who might use this bomb; he is also the representative of a mankind which, for its own good, ought not to live. Well, you may say, let us punish him, eradicate him, reduce him to fertilizer in his own Belsen ovens. But before we agree, let us ask two questions.

First, is not our society populated by millions who share the views of the young totalitarian? "Shall we say there is no such thing as truth and error, but that anything is truth to a man which he troweth?" Newman asked many years ago. Undoubtedly, on the score of ethics, a vast number of people would reply in the affirmative, claiming the right to possess tomorrow a truth wholly different from that of which they boast today, if a change be profitable to themselves.

Second, on what ground shall we denounce the young totalitarian? As modern men we have said that our knowledge of psychology is so extensive that there is no way of attributing to any individual responsibility for his actions. With the benevolent Mr. Justice Holmes we have declared that the assumption of a persistent, functioning, spiritual nature in man, regally entitled to live not by nature's laws, but by the rights rooted in the order of its being, is untenable obfuscation; and that all so-called rights have merely been staked out by social agreement so as to make the business of survival possible. Arthur Koestler has recently quoted Professor J. W. Bernal to the effect that because "collective action is the only effective action, it is the only virtuous action"; and has gone on to note correctly that on the basis of such a philosophy the young totalitarian must be a virtuous person, since all he has done is to subordinate his individual rectitude to the purposes of the effective collectivity.

In short, our millstones seem now to have brought us to the point where simple justice and simple logic compel us to say to the *Schutzstaffel* trooper on trial that since "one world" is the sole absolute because it is the ultimate collectivity, and since man knows so much about everything that he can know nothing, then the only reason why he, the trooper, is being tried is because in the struggle for ultimate mastery of the "one world" he lost. And to one's horror—though it may well be horror only for those who conserve a nostalgic reverence for the ancient ethical traditions of mankind—one must observe that this is just what is being said. Mr. Justice Jackson's corpus of ex post facto law would not be objectionable if it were limited to emphasis on universally evident principles which by mere chance had not been written into statute. Thus there would be honor in trying men reputed to be responsible for the torture inflicted at Buchenwald, even if humanity had never previously reckoned with such camps and so had failed to legislate against what was done in them. But Mr. Justice Jackson's law is not limited—it is rather whatever one wishes to put into the code. It has decreed, for example, that aggression against Poland was a crime against international justice, for which the guilty must be punished. But if aggression against Poland was criminal, then Russia, too, was guilty. And how can the guilty sit in judgment without making of the trial a notorious farce?

Let us probe more deeply into ourselves and hide nothing. During thousands of years of recorded history, the noblest among men struggled to conserve justice. They husbanded what they had of it with greater care than they expended on their flocks or their clothing or their food. One cannot read the Mosaic books or Plato's *Laws* or Aristotle's *Ethics* or the Epistles of St. Paul or the sermons of Savonarola or the writings of Thomas More without becoming deeply aware that for these authors justice was a more fearful and dangerous, a more potentially useful and beneficent thing than atomic energy is for us. They saw that if any large number of men began seriously to sanction injustice, the common bonds of humanity would be riven asunder.

And we? Must not any observer say of us that although we train multitudes of men and women to use social, political, and scientific energy hitherto unknown, we give only a handful of them any lessons whatsoever in justice? Indeed, do we not cheerfully admit that we do not know what justice is? When we dropped conflagrations on the women and children of Nagasaki and Hiroshima, were our leaders pacing the floor in the night wondering whether such a gruesome massacre could be justified? Did we tell our armies of occupation, when they went out to do what might have been their sacred duty, that they were to put on the armor of justice? The stern truth is that their leaders did not know what the armor of justice might be.

And because these things are so, the words we have spoken in reply to the totalitarians have no fire in them. Why should we have imagined that we could blot out the influence of the evil genius of Goebbels—for he was both evil and a genius—with clichés, the meaning of which we ourselves had not explored? Nothing ever said to nurse the sorrow of bruised and bleeding humanity back to health was more like balm than was the language of the Atlantic Charter. It was the blueprint of a liberating social vision by which men might have steered a course onward. But who, if perchance he even recalls that such words were spoken (it is part of the tawdriness of our estate that apparently they were never written), does not bear heavily his unconfessed guilt for not having insisted that they must not be forgotten? Now we say nothing any more because we have nothing to say. We have had an incomparable, a liberating, victory, but we remember it only in phrases so tawdry, stilted, and unctuous that it would be better for us if we were silent.

Indeed, if one looks realistically at this victory in its present outline, expecting no more than the Stoic, for instance, might in his day have expected of a comparable triumph, one finds it difficult to think of any image save that of a pit into which a crumbling civilization is falling deeper, hour by hour. In his day Fénelon, aghast at battles which were merely battles and at victories which were only victories, wrote, at some peril, to his master, the King of France: "We are in real need of only one thing. That one thing is called justice! The fact that you must protect the boundaries of the realm is by no manner of means a reason why you should take from the neighbor of France his terrain." And I do not believe that any of us can legitimately surmise that the great bishop, whose concern for righteousness was no more academic or merely theological than was that of Socrates, would have spoken any differently to the masters of our time.

This, then, is where we stand in our debate with the young totalitarian. He is the beaten inheritor of an era; we are still that era's victims. Or rather, we stand like policemen at a crowded corner in the world's history, ourselves rendered powerless in the traffic snarl. Somehow we must make up our minds to get out of it. We must find a call, an order, a drift, a motive. But where, you will ask, shall we discover any of these? The American scholar would be false to his tradition if he asserted that this is an easy question. He has lived so long at his job of digging after truth that the discovery of a world round about him in which ethical truth no longer exists is a startling one, indeed. It is clear to him that without such a truth there is no defense against totalitarianism. But where is he to find it?

I shall say some things first of all concerning the scientist. He is the inner motor impulse of our time, but not its maker. The function of his method in the realm of ethical thinking has been to correct the bad guesses and facile generalizations of moral theoreticians about the nature of the physical universe. But that the scientist himself should contribute constructively to ethical theory, to the discussion of the nature and the ultimate destiny of man, is another question. It may well be that his comments on these subjects will merely arouse irony comparable to that which the moralist evoked when he indulged in fantasies on scientific topics.

Again, it is no longer certain that the people would follow science if it attempted to lead them. The average man has never wanted to be a scientist. What he has craved is the pleasant fruits of scientific labor; and he does not even yet realize that it is he himself who turns these good things into fearful weapons of disaster. Before Nagasaki, the great men of the laboratory were held to be humanity's servants. Today that is no longer so.

Finally, the scientist has not been taken at his true worth. Nothing could be more striking than is the resemblance between the faces of devoted chemists and biologists and the countenances of zealous practitioners of the spiritual life. In both one reads the acceptance of renunciation which is the first principle of the vitality of mind. When Franicis of Assisi came down from Monte Alverno to die, there were in his hands and his feet the stigmata, or signs, of liberating spiritual suffering. And partly because of him, I reverence an illustrious scientific worker I know in whose flesh mysterious rays have left their ominous imprint—secular stigmata—or are they secular?

The scientist and St. Francis! I propose that duality to education as a point of departure for getting out of the abyss. Why should we always think of what the scientist does and never of what he is? The inventions of technology are only gadgets, just as the concept of the United Nations is a gadget of political scientists. But that a scholar should, by reason of delving sacrificially into the secrets of nature, come to live by a purifying and ennobling law—that the great scientist is, in short, a kind of saint—happens to be a wonderful truth. It proves that something can really be done to rid man of his dross. I have known, as have you, eminent workers who by dint of contemplating the fateful definiteness of the natural law became even as little children despite the vastness of the vistas which their intellects had conjured up. They may never have spoken the name of God, but the splendor of His handiwork was reflected in the humility of their eyes.

Theirs is not spurious mysticism, like that of the Nazi or the Communist, but comes right out of the heart of Reality. It is the most impressive result of being a scientist, though it does not follow from the use of scientific method. And why should we not believe that it is quite as possible to transform man through contemplation of the moral law—of the order by which the human spirit moves to its fruition, and from which it can deviate only with disaster? It is true that this order is even more difficult to discern than is the rule which governs the stars. The saint, who for the sake of reading it aright has hovered over the crater in the surface of the human soul, may see through a glass darkly; but he sees. And in seeing, he too garners into his own personal vision a goodness which is a reflection of everlasting Goodness.

Thus the scientist and the saint meet at a point of light. The difference between them is, however, great. The saint is he who has made the fundamental assent, namely, that to holiness, which is the immolation of self for the sake of integration with the Whole. He is not a variety of religious experience, but a continuous, living, spiritual experiment. Holiness is, whether one relishes it or not, a fact. It is, I grant, terrifying and uncomfortable. So also is the burden of integrity, or of persecution suffered for justice's sake. The people have always been fearful of the saint. They are afraid he will take their toys away. But they ask nevertheless for the sacrifice, the heroism, the unworldliness of saints, so that life as a whole may preserve an inner core of decency.

There is no ethic which can resist the solvents of totalitarianism save one that is rooted in holiness. No one has ever known that better than the Nazis knew it. Justice can no more thrive without the saint than our knowledge of the physical universe can thrive without the scientist. He is the one who knows that justice cannot derive from an armistice between omnipresent protagonists in the struggle for existence. It must either come out of the character of the universe or be the arbitrary product of the human will. Lord Acton's phrase, "All power corrupts, and absolute power corrupts absolutely," was never more true than it is here; for if man has the power to create an ethic after his own liking, that power is absolute and will corrupt absolutely. It always has done so.

I should like to add two things. To ask the saint and the scientist to give an account of themselves is not to suggest that either will immediately be believed. For those of us to whom the ancient Jewish and Christian faith brings not defeat but joy, not doubt but confidence, it may be difficult to understand why the urge to holiness which glows so warm in our tradition should be invisible to so many. The Christian is aware that the Beatitudes, eight in number like a round of dancers, are fruits that swing too high in the tree for him to pluck. None the less, it seems to him that nothing more glorious was ever said of man than that some day his reach might attain even unto them—that he might be rich because he was poor and mighty because he was humbly selfless. But he must be patient. He cannot help knowing that a curtain has fallen between him and the rest of men. He must give them an example before he can furnish them with a doctrine.

Again, there is no point in being led into a debate about whether ours is a sensate culture. Of course there are ominous signs of degeneration. Paul Bourget wrote of the French eighteenth century:

Men and women moved about amid intellectualized fantasies, without any inkling of daily and dolorous reality. Where could they have learned that the world was tormented by the struggle for daily bread when they came and went in the midst of unbridled luxury and exorbitant privilege, themselves light-o'-loves and fondlers of abstractions?

And one need scarcely wonder that we should be fashioning our own plaster casts of the *ancien regime*. Ours, too, is a small but gaudily tinted society of women who desire to be not sweet but acrid, and who with their shifting men drape their lusts behind a screen of kaleidoscopic legality; of the male hard of heart, aloof from all interests save those of money and the ironic emptiness of the passions it will sate; and of an omnipresent bordel of the mind, wherein a pantomime of the breasts of courtesans blots out not merely the remembrance of mortality but the torch of life itself. But I think that if we can once more find out which end of the universe is up and which down, these things will matter little.

It will, perhaps, suffice for our time if there can be found room inside our education for so much of the teaching of justice and charity as will enable our children to build dikes against the flooding of the spirit of man. If we can put together for them what the scientist knows about the meaning of life and what the mystic and the saint know—it is very little and yet infinitely difficult to come by, even so—they may be strong and comforted in their awareness that the true unity that underlies human experience is not cosmic fact but universal mystery, though it is a mystery that has a stern orderliness which the mind can conceive, as well as a seemingly wayward, but nevertheless also carefully patterned, goodness which we can call Love. They will not have Truth, but they will know with the great Greek that "Truth for all time abideth."

WHAT IS EDUCATION?*

"TRUTH," SAID PESTALOZZI THE OPTIMIST, INDICATING THEREWITH his approach to education, "is a medicine which takes hold." This metaphor appears to find wide endorsement. The pragmatist may have his version of "truth," and the Thomist another, but they seem to agree here, even if (to venture a debatable generalization) the first judges by the value of the medicine and the second by the value of the truth. Pessimists also appear not to dissent, save when they are devotees of total negation; and it is to them one naturally turns for comment on the ills of our time. "There is in man," Georges Bernanos wrote, "a secret and incomprehensible hatred, not only of his fellowman but of himself." This hatred, thought to be more than a mere absence of love, is thus viewed as the hidden malignant malady of the human will, and truth flowering in affection alone can cure it. For H. G. Wells, on the other hand, as his final treatise reveals, man's tragic difficulty lies in his mind's inability to adapt itself to the constantly changing conditions that result from its own inventiveness. He has gone into the cellars of nature and come up with its headiest wine. But he cannot cope with the power intoxication that this induces. This view, if correct, would seem to suggest that one kind of truth at least is a fateful poison. The medicine has taken hold, but it is evil. Therefore, unless there be another kind of truth no antidote can be found.

Should we not then say, somewhat tritely, that the schools must seek what man tries to find? And if we discuss education in such a context, should we not consider what it is as a process

---

* Reprinted from *Daedalus: Journal of the American Academy of Arts and Sciences* 88 (1959), pp. 25–39.

before we attempt to define its concern with truth? At any rate, this is what we shall proceed to do. The schools constitute a kind of arc, the extremities of which are rooted in wholly disparate functions. At the outset, the teacher is a person who tells children what it is considered desirable they should know—verbal symbols, the multiplication table, the names of rivers and seas, and phrases expressing civic, ethical, and religious beliefs. A little later there will be consideration of what Paul Weiss calls "the mastery of techniques"—of diction and reckoning, of accuracy, of the progression of thought from data to conclusions. At the other end of the academic span there is, however, in principle no concern with the imparting of knowledge. The scholar in his study, the monk in his cell, the scientist in his laboratory—if you will, the poet under his tree—for all of these the dialogue is starkly between the self and Reality. Moses is on his mountain, Pascal in his room. To make such conversation possible in terms of scholarship may well be the central assignment of the university. And if one would see what the cost is, inside or outside of academic walls, one has only to study the lives of four men who perhaps best represent the aspirations of modernity—van Gogh, Kierkegaard, Einstein, and Planck. Only gradually, sometimes with agonizing slowness, will the thrill and the terror of discovery, or pseudo-discovery, be communicated and begin to travel back over the line of the arc. Some discovered values never disappear from education, and others do not enter into its purview at all.

Between the grade school and the research institute lie the reaches of education in which there takes place a sort of fusion between exploration shared and knowledge imparted. The reputable college, for example, must at least upon occasion be akin to Augustine's *Cassiciacum*, where in goodly fellowship problems like that of "the happy life" were discussed in the give and take of dialogue. Yet even the best of such institutions will normally be busy with things thought rather than with man thinking. Carlyle held that one must be content with enough happiness to get one's work done. Manifestly, education in its intermediate stages keeps busy giving young people sufficient knowledge (and it may be insufficient wisdom) to perform useful service in the world. Catering to utility, as a matter of fact, may tempt the fully academic mind to derisory or even ribald comment. But if all of us on campuses are quite honest, will we not admit that a great deal of what we do is cognate in character and purpose?

At any rate, scrutiny will reveal how closely the three concerns—knowledge, inquiry, and usefulness—are intertwined. A great many young women, for instance, are trained to teach in nursery and grade schools. I think it quite probable that my own college, while little more than a secondary school, was graduating teachers fully as able to impart the kind of instruction needed as it is now doing when it has become a sedate and rather exacting college of liberal arts. Why not? If your task is to teach addition and subtraction, you need to know about these and not about the calculus, which is in the course of study only because it is believed to give the student as a person insight into an aspect of Reality that she will then know about but not use. Even more notable is the fact that we have added to the training program a great deal of information about theoretical and applied psychology. Obviously this, whatever its value, is not supposed to be taught in turn. It is part of the course of study because of our hope that when the teacher has learned something of what research workers have found out about children, she will see these in a broader and clearer perspective than would otherwise be the case.

Nor is the situation fundamentally very different with college teaching, though at first sight it may seem otherwise. No one has as yet proved, or is likely to do so, that there is any genuine relationship between earning a doctorate by writing a treatise on the sources of *Samson Agonistes* and teaching a course in Milton to juniors. Granted a reasonable amount of aesthetic intelligence, one no doubt could manage a wholly satisfactory semester with only the text and a convenient manual. The academic accessories probably do little more than befog the student's mind. But the fact that the instructor has the long trek to the doctorate behind him does, unless he be a dolt, enable him and his students to see each other in a wholly different and more invigorating light than either would otherwise manage, for through this companionship a young man at a desk will gain some insight into the processes of the exploration of the knowable. Fichte thus instructed the scholar: He "is to forget what he has accomplished as soon as it is accomplished, and is to think constantly of what he must still do." To have lived for some time in communion with such a scholar will be for many a young person as exhilarating, and one must immediately add as humbling, as standing on a Darien peak.

It appears unlikely that the situation is wholly different insofar as other callings are concerned. A candidate for appointment to the foreign service will have to know whatever that service at the time deems important, including how to write and speak a foreign language. But having painfully mastered Spanish, he will normally find himself in Timbukto or Saigon as a vice-consul, dutifully writing out visa prescriptions or practicing minor roles in the eternal drama of commerce. The average chemist will become a member of some chain gang of scientists marshaled like a posse for ferreting out a new explosive or antibiotic. And the political scientist, fresh from the study of the arcana of government, will be fortunate if he can pass a civil service examination and proceed daily to chores with the Housing Authority or the Bureau of the Budget. But if somewhere along the road such a student has caught a glimpse of the "city" as seen by a man for whom the span between Plato and Quincy Wright does not exhaust the vision of that "city" as it has been or may be, he will not sleep without dreams.

I believe we may therefore conclude that as education proceeds it does not lose sight of the purposiveness implicit in its beginnings—namely the imparting of knowledge—but will, when it is wisely conceived, also reckon constantly with the ultimate objective, which is sharing the life of the scholar, poet, and saint. As a matter of fact, it will be driven to do so by the passion of the best students it serves. These will question the knowledge of their teachers but never the awe of them as they stand on the brink of discovery. Thoreau in his time asked whether Concord could not "hire some Abelard to lecture us." The query seems to be universal, save possibly when men have become uninhibitedly utilitarian. It seeks wisdom for the many through the contemplation of the one. And whether the answer be given in terms of experimental science, or in those of the speculative intellect as with the Greeks, or in those of the prophecy embedded in the Hebraic tradition, or in those of mysticism either Christian or Oriental, it will be in the final analysis the celestial fruit of a wedding between the "I" and the "Thou," to use Martin Buber's pertinent phrasing. We begin with the communication to others of the easily known in order that at long last we may find ourselves closeted with the unknown. Only if we are so placed, at least waveringly, hesitatingly, fleetingly, can we mortal beings acquire the sense of comedy and tragedy, of the holy and the profane, that gives us the stature to which it is our destiny to aspire.

Perhaps we may now venture to define the liberal arts as follows: a course of study designed to encourage tentatively integrated learning about man's most fruitful insights into himself and the reality about him, so that a student may feel the texture of the known in order to be able to realize, sooner or later, that this is only the garment of the unknown. If the known were the whole of being, we should have no answer to Newman's question about Scaliger: How could so much learning have passed through the mind of one man—and why did it pass? Aquinas in his day held that the ultimate properties of being must remain unknown, just as the potential existence of a human creature cannot cease to be enigmatical. To think of molecular movement going on constantly inside a baseball thrown to a hitter is merely to tease oneself out of thought. If the psychiatrist could map out his patient's psyche, the therapeutic task would be less impossible. He cannot do so. In the final analysis there is relatively little we can really know of other men, save that we aspire to the truth about them.

Let me add a few comments that regrettably are more addicted to the vice of generalization than could be wished. First, the educator must realize that what the storerooms of the past contain is indispensable treasure. Of necessity he will challenge the accusation of pedantry constantly leveled against him, but he cannot function unless this charge is in some measure justified. He must have books about him that few other men read. The genesis and progression of ideas he will observe with a reverence other men do not feel. Indeed, one may go so far as to say that the great teacher has a genuine affection for the past, which makes the sharp lighting up of any of its moods or features a memorable experience. But he must avoid like the plague every form of dotage leading to the assumption that he or any other human being exists for the sake of knowing what is already known. How often, indeed, does research undertaken by the fraternity of educators seem a tedious adding up of figures in old ledgers!

One need not assert that it is valueless even so, but the teaching scholar will not live for his students if he be merely afraid of becoming an unwise virgin with no oil in the lamp. Yesterday must be for him the coast line on which he can stand before plunging into the unplummeted and perilous sea of tomorrow. Therefore, secondly, education must accept as a kind of law that even the rediscovery of the past must have relevance for the present. A man will be worth his salt if he sees quite clearly that his life will be worth while only if at some moment at least he is visited by a creative and illuminating intuition of reality, personal and not mimicked. This, I think, can be seen occurring again and again in the experience of Whitehead or Hocking, but it is no doubt the fire that brings wisdom into being wherever it is enkindled. At any rate, age is meaningless if this virility be present in the teacher, and that youth knows instinctively. Thus gifted, the scholar will realize that Kierkegaard's grasp of the meaning of Hegel, or Einstein's insight into the principles of relativity, came to them as young men. He will not disparage what is called the "creative," though he will cling to his role of critic. Because he himself has passed through the open door of the mind, he will respect pioneer intellectual effort, no matter how seemingly revolutionary or unexpected the forward thrust may be.

It follows that education is in part the preservation not merely of what has been learned but also of the traditions, the methods, of learning. These are several, not singular. No doubt a major educational mishap has been the assumption that the always salutary debate about what should be selected for the classroom from the vast accumulation of the known involves agreement as to a certain formula for learning to know it. There are educators whose pedagogical dogmas brook no criticism. But as a matter of fact one individual's best way of learning may be quite different from another's. One nation, to some extent conditioned by historical environment, will not learn most adequately in the same way another nation does. We may note in passing that this is probably the principal discovery made by the Soviets in their satellite areas. Why should anybody take it for granted that all teachers must subscribe, for their souls' salvation, to a single formula? But if any teacher be a canny person, he will certainly weigh methods that have proved useful for other teachers, and he will be as objective in evaluating them as a purchasing agent is when examining samples of leather. He will consider the advice of Comenius and Kirchensteiner, Loyola and Dewey, Ulich and Livingstone. It will not occur to him that all sound educating is contained in an approximation to a full comprehension of one aspect of education.

Therewith we come to the meaning of the terms in Pestalozzi's maxim. What shall we say about truth? And what about the medicine that takes hold? In other words, how shall education conceive of the real and the good? What then is truth? You will not expect me to put the questions in terms of philosophical inquiry, as if perchance I felt able to improve upon Spinoza. What will be under discussion here is this: When education declares that its function is to find and to teach truth, to what is it committing itself? The completely frank answer in terms of the actual existing situation is: to not very much. There are vast numbers of students and teachers, at all academic levels, for whom the task assigned is merely to absorb and emit a specified quantity of information, in the hope that a sufficient amount will be retained by the student to make possible his academic survival after examination. Of course it is expected that the data imparted will be reasonably accurate from the giver's and the receiver's point of view—that the class will not say *le escargots* or assert that Shakespeare began his career by writing *The Tempest*. Therewith truth has become accuracy in the mnemonic reproduction of determinable data. It is of considerable interest to note that the majority of the vocal critics of our schools are like most of those schools' supporters in seeming not to want more of education than this. The difference between them is merely one of emphasis on certain facts as being more valuable than others.

It is probably evident from what has been said that this version of "truth" seems inadequate to me, though I should not wish to be thought ignoring the kernel of realism that is in it. Nor does it seem less injudicious to isolate, as some have, what Pestalozzi may have meant by "medicine." To assume that "good citizens" can be made to emerge from the schools as hot cross buns do from a bakery is to take a benign view indeed of human nature and the teaching profession. This happens to be what never happens. To be sure, good schools are often effective conditioning devices. If youngsters can be induced to absorb moral maxims into their blood streams at a sufficiently early age, the effect may be relatively lasting. But in this realm it is especially pertinent to bear in mind Heidegger's phrase, *das im Sagen Ungesagte*—that which the sayer has not said. The moral *paideia* of the schools will congeal in the psyches of young scholars like a lump of indigestible fat in the pottage unless it can be fused with the drift of the intellect and the genuine drive of the will. Character is never formed as aught save conscience; and this is not a recipe book but a living commitment to sublimation of the self. That most reasonably gifted men and women wish to make that commitment is, I think, fortunately true. Yet all experience seems to indicate that what can be done from without to intensify this desire and direct it to good ends—that is, by the family, the school, and the church—is to awaken joy and pride in belonging. A youngster who is jubilantly confident of the stature of his preparatory school will wish to be worthy of it, and this longing may endure through life. And it seems indubitable that the influence of the church is proportionate to its ability to evoke affectionate trust in its practice of the holy life. This may seem as if man were here being doomed to becoming "organization man." Aristotle long since so doomed him, as the evidence required. What alone matters is the quality of his gregariousness.

"Truth" as education must conceive of it is, then, primarily awareness of the vital activity of the receptive, creative human mind face to face with reality in the whole of its illusory overtness and its revealing concealment. It is on the one hand "man thinking" and on the other that which can be seized and held in thought. "Truth" therefore cannot be for any wise teacher merely "what he troweth," to borrow Newman's words, because while awareness must be vividly personal it is nevertheless bound to the whole with hoops firmer than steel. Here is a brief comment on a characteristic, though not always recognized, trait of Aquinas taken from a recent book by Josef Pieper:**

The same intrepidity made him ask, in his *Commentary on the Book of Job*, whether Job's conversation with the Lord God did not violate reverence—to which he gave the almost outrageous answer that truth does not change according to the standing of the person to whom it is addressed. He who speaks truthfully is invulnerable, no matter who may be his adversary.

What is here meant by "truth" is a firm grip on some part of reality. The earth does spin round; there was a process of evolution, though we may never fully know how it operated. The right to discover and report such truths is the most inviolable of rights. But if a man proceeds to assert that any part of the true

** Josef Pieper, *The Silence of St. Thomas*, translated by John Murray, s. j., Daniel O'Connor (New York: Pantheon Books, Inc., 1957), pp. 20–21.

is the whole, if he construes his article as being the encyclopedia, he is as gravely in error as would be the planner who believed that if he built a city of skyscrapers there would be no traffic problem.

Accordingly, here are the poles between which education moves in practice: the scholar's free, creative, but rigorously controlled awareness of the cosmic or human verity that he holds with awe in his hands, and his humble, submissive realization that this little, precious though it be, is only like one of the diamonds on Cecil Rhodes' plain. This is why, to think in contemporary terms, it is utterly senseless and life-destroying to hold that education can be either purely scientific or not concerned with science. In the wake of the eerie excitement caused by Russia's ability to push a satellite into outer space, we seemed for a time wholly to forget that for years education in the United States has been veering strongly to a one-sided concern with engineering and other forms of applied science, and that we were in grave danger of losing our collective dedication to the deeper forms of contemplation, whether they were concerned with mathematics or psychoanalysis, metaphysics or pure poetry. Having been told over and over again that the United States could have sent a rocket to the moon years ago had it been so minded and willing to foot the bill, why should we now imagine that safety can be found only in thicker dabs of science on the schoolboy's bread?

The reason why the veering alluded to has taken place is of course this: The impact of scientific discovery on our modes of living is so great that we are all caught up into a Heraclitean world. Cellulose fiber makes growing cotton on sun-parched fields a dubiously profitable venture, and vegetable oils deprive the cow of a major reason for being. Indeed, one by one the animals become superfluous save when dead. I can think of no statement that more vividly indicates the change that has already taken place in the human environment. It would be incredibly stupid of the educator not to do what he can to make young scholars aware of the steps by which the mind of man has moved thus far. Yet who can doubt that a stern appraisal of our people's ability to live in the world that is now its companion, day in and out, will reveal equally glaring weaknesses—widespread inability to cope with the leisure that is the by-product of technology, and a resulting softness of mind, heart, and hand; the lack of impulse to enter into the cultural worlds of other peoples, past and present, that has so often led to manifestations of puerile gullibility or assumed superiority, or (what is even worse) to the isolation of the American in environments that he has been expected to influence or indeed improve; and above all a hankering after spurious kinds of "peace of mind," as if these might not prove to be the ultimate enfeebling narcotics.

If what has been said is in a measure correct, a number of conclusions are suggested, some few of which will be advanced here with the requisite intrepidity.

First, it must be obvious that education can proceed in its full glory and significance only insofar as it is concerned with those for whom it is not merely an obligation, to be met by trudging more or less wearily to school, but also primarily and increasingly an adventure. Young scholars must be chosen and not simply endured. While Maritain and the Harvard report on *General Education in a Free Society* are right in holding that some measure of liberal education is the privilege of all citizens, it remains as certain as anything can well be that even in the most democratic of societies many will fail to move beyond the stage at which knowledge is communicated fact, either because they are unable to do so or because the journey does not interest them. Those who are eager and able to embark on the *adventure* of education should be singled out as soon as possible, freed of crippling economic handicaps, and made to realize that the training of the mind is at least as rigorous as the training of the body. To continue to accept the lowest common pupil denominator as the norm is to doom the potential intellectual power of the nation to turning somersaults around the statue of Huckleberry Finn.

One happy result of emphasis on pupil selectivity would be that at long last we should be able to train teachers in a relatively rational manner. There are candidites for the profession able and willing to go with unquenchable enthusiasm to the task of guiding the unfolding creative mind. Others will be more at home with the larger numbers for whom awakened interest is the only lure. And there will be some who, sensing perhaps a vocation akin to that of nursing, will concern themselves with young people who are in a sense anormal, because of either handicaps or some lesion of the will. As things are now, exception having duly been made for the most fortunate of colleges and preparatory schools, no teacher working at a level below that of the university can tell what it is he is expected to accomplish. He will know only that his work is with youth and he usually will find himself in as impossible a situation as is the driver of a twenty-four-mule team some of whose charges are halt and lame while others are eager for the road. It is no wonder that problems of teacher morale exist, particularly in schools compelled to assemble in the same rooms youngsters who should no doubt be in jail and the sons and daughters of parents who have long been devotedly interested in the progress of the human intelligence.

Some clarification of what is meant by the freedom of the teacher seems highly desirable at this point. What Aquinas and many others have said about the inviolability of the mind when it is aware of truth must be supported, even when the cost is as tragically heavy as it has been in Hungary. This freedom is the inner radiance of every free society. It is the "single string," to use Donne's phrase, that cements scholar and teacher in comradeship and mutual respect. But one cannot conclude that the same freedom should be claimed for the imparting of information *unless this is actually the communication of truth in the sense defined*. The assertion may need a word of comment. For instance, the historian who might contend that the Roman *limes* was a deposit of quicklime should be free to say so only until somebody finds him out. Or again, a mathematician who has not in a measure kept abreast of developments in his field can hardly claim a natural right to remain in a state of ignorance. But a student of the Roman past who advances a new hypothesis concerning the nature and functions of the *limes* based on evidence fresh or old must have complete freedom to publish it, no matter how startling the contentions or how inconclusive the argument may seem. Failure to make this distinction, admittedly difficult to arrive at though it be in concrete instances, is responsible for a widespread reputable skepticism about academic freedom. This failure is no doubt rooted in a too uncritical readiness to apply standards indispensable for research to the lower schools. One may argue that this is the less dangerous course. Yet the fact remains that the maxim, "Once a teacher, always a teacher," regardless of quality, performance, or vigorous elation, is unquestionably a reason why the profession of teaching has fallen into some disrepute. Is it not more injurious than the difference between the salary paid to the president of Amherst College and that of the chairman of General Motors?

Conversely, the proper freedom of a pupil does not consist in doing what he wishes. I am persuaded that, once young people have progressed beyond the years with which Madame Montessori was concerned, they rather wistfully expect someone to tell them what to do and how. This does not mean, to be sure, that they will wear hair shirts with pleasure. But few statements can be made with greater assurance (or have so been made) than that pupil satisfaction and response are far greater in exacting high schools like Hunter or Brooklyn Technical than they are in makeshift mental factories for which the football season is the major academic event. But there is a kind of freedom at higher levels to which the fledgling young scholar has every right to lay claim. This is on the one hand freedom to respect as a person, regardless of his ancestry or the affiliations of his family. The right to gross discourtesy is not one of the attributes of the teaching profession. On the other hand, the student should have the feeling that his own dawning awareness of part of reality will be accorded mature critical respect. Who has really learned to teach who has not at some time realized that a young mind can light up a scene that has hitherto been dark? When I dealt with a class concerned with some aspects of English verse, it was not a commentary by a distinguished critic that I used to clarify a stanza by Marvell but an essay written by a Harvard senior.

It is at this point that the marvelous utility of student discussion should be adduced. Young people do not suffer one another's foolishness gladly. Indeed, they are loath to accept the mutual exchange of wisdom. Very rarely can a college student talk as an equal with a teacher. He can speak at, back to, about, around a revered instructor; but the generations dig their moats and lower only certain drawbridges. Each young person dealing with others, however, under the aegis of education, has in the company of his fellows a priceless abrasiveness, a hugging and pushing aside, an abrupt and vigorous way of proceeding from enmity to affection and back again, which are all like sprouting combative antlers of the mind. How good and fruitful the college campus is (as Newman indicated a century ago) on which thought etches itself out in jagged contour during student debate! Can we not all look back gratefully and see ourselves limping by reason of the bruises earned in such struggles and the depths that had to be leaped over, but still having in the end weary but exhilarated companionship? Alas that we should lose this skill later on! I am sadly reminded that in the days of yore Henry Mencken and Stuart Sherman, the first a stout brew of Nietzsche and *Simplicissimus*, the second a glass of pure humanistic port, were wont to assail each other with uninhibited vehemence. It was not a pleasant spectacle for anyone who liked them both, for neither was any longer young. But if I had my way no student would graduate who had not had a similar glorious row at some time.

Finally there is the harassing but unavoidable ground on which "truth" and "medicine" meet. The educated person will not always be driven by inherited impulses or find himself unable to get away from the screen on which are flashed pictures of his subconscious mind. Virtues, whether of the practical or speculative life, are disciplines. The Latin-speaking students of Aristotle referred to each of these as *habitudo*, as a form of thought and action to which one voluntarily has grown accustomed. For the great Greek, even as for Confucius, wisdom could never be synonymous with knowledge. The knower might be all else than wise in his knowing. There is no graver peril to which modern man can be exposed than surmising that *phronesis* is automatically built into his practical application of the insights that he has acquired. As he succumbs to this error, he becomes a thing that can be used rather than a man deciding of what use he can be. This we have seen with implacable clarity in the moral callousness of the gifted—scientists and engineers, jurists and writers—who have served tyrants. We shall see it even more plainly in the manipulation of minds by new and subtler forms of propaganda.

On what basic convictions the commitment to virtue is to rest becomes therewith the query that must be put, even though the answers given may prove so stormily different that many will turn aside persuaded that life is too brief to justify the quest of a decision. I shall say no more here than to remind you that Max Planck, under the torment of nazism, joined Newman in believing education without theology incomplete. Assuredly this affords one gateway to the final dialogue between oneself and reality. That dialogue will have for its theme where the last boundary is, what foundation lies below the deepest cellar into which we can look. Perhaps a man will decide that there is neither boundary nor fundament. A large number have so concluded. The "disinherited mind," of which Erich Heller speaks, indeed seems, oddly enough, the response of the intellectual West to the great Christians of the Russian East, alive in the days before a sinister form of dialectic made its successful bid for power. The conviction that we are of the warp and woof of the here and now, and have no wedding garment for a feast elsewhere, has been freely arrived at by men of genius. The university must respect their testimony. It must have full liberty to attest to that respect.

But if education is to be what I have said it is, namely "awareness of the vital activity of the receptive, creative mind face to face with reality in the whole of its illusory overtness and its revealing concealment," how can it complete its assignment unless it throws light from every available source on the questions asked by Albert Einstein eight years ago about modern scientific man: "Has he not in an effort characterized by being intellectual only forgotten his responsibilty and his dignity? A man who is inwardly free and loyal to his conscience can, it is true, be destroyed, but he cannot be turned into a slave or a blind tool." These things Max Horkheimer had in mind when, returning to Germany from exile to become rector of the bombed-out University of Frankfurt, he etablished chairs of Protestant and Catholic theology without being personally a devotee of either. He believed that some light might be cast on the queries of Einstein by a discipline that has played and still plays a mighty role in the drama of the West. Most assuredly he was not thinking of an acrimonious debating society, nor did he acquire one. The European university seems to realize, far better than our truncated experience will permit, that a theological faculty consists of educated men and not of self-appointed functionaries either in a kind of hypothetical Office of the Inquisition or in a club of intellectuals the primary activity of which is to blackball the parson.

It is not too much to say that the immaturity, or it might be better to say the incompleteness, of American culture manifests itself at no point so clearly as it does when religious issues are under discussion. There are many reasons why this is so, but the principal one undoubtedly is that theology has been studied so far away from the main stream of university life. Quite without knowing it, we have agreed with Tito and Rákosi in banning religion to the rectory. Therefore Catholic theologians are widely and falsely identified in the public mind with rigorous censorship, while Protestants, with comparable absurdity, are deemed to be a dwindling hortatory minority who have not made up their minds whether God exists or not. As for the antitheologians, need one refrain from saying that their inability to span the gulfs that stretch between themselves is no less scandalous than is the scandal of religious divisiveness? The statement that a faculty of theology must include representatives of every form of theology

—thus identifying the proposed venture with absurdity—is admittedly difficult to confute. But it is perhaps in reality no more arresting than would be the contention that an antitheological faculty of philosophy must include every kind of antitheologian.

The fact of the matter is that thinking in theological terms, even amidst the turmoil of recent social tragedy, has attained heights of pertinence and influence that cannot be whisked out of being. It is at least probable that the books of Père Teilhard de Chardin will outlive those of Sartre. I shall say no more than that I find myself wishing American education could face the ultimate questions concerning the nature of human existence with the same willingness to discuss the whole of the evidence that I find elsewhere in the world. The numerous deep-rooted atavistic impulses with which many American scholars embark on life do not seem a replica of the Great Wall. I shall confess that to me it appears rather odd that we may all be blown to kingdom come because of some resolve to end the debate about power powerfully, before the American university has a fair chance to talk about whether man is immortal. Not that a faculty resolution on the subject would be particularly reassuring. But at least if I were a young, inquisitive person, I should prefer to be slain on such a tremendous scene after having weighed all the evidence concerning my survival. It seems a pity to deprive the fledgling American intellectual of that opportunity.

THE NEW SCHOOLBOY'S
SHINING FACE*

AMONG INNUMERABLE PRIVATE CAPSULE DEFINITIONS OF EDUCATION,
I find my own and, frankly, rather like it. Schools and similar
institutions exist to impart information, to form habits of intellectual accuracy, and to foster judgment—moral, aesthetic and
prudential. There is nothing specially glamorous about such a
pedagogical platform, but if its precepts could be put into practice in any genuinely effective way, mankind would no doubt
prove to be rather superior to what it is now. At any rate it
may be interesting to consider what is the present state of education ten years after the end of cataclysm which had the
extraordinary effect of concentrating the human scene, in a
world-wide sense, and very greatly reducing it in size. What had
thitherto been culturally exotic now began to be superseded for
the imagination by the culturally uniform. Emphasis was no
longer placed on who does voodoo dances and where, but rather
on who can read and write, work a Worthington pump, and
keep the flies away from the meat in the butcher shop. The impact of this change in orientation on certain great civilizations
is quite evident and amazing. Mysterious China suddenly stopped
repeating the maxims of Confucius and placating ancestral spirits.
At least it has done so in public, being now committed to repeating phrases about capitalism, class warfare, imperialism, and
the glories of industrial production, which ten years ago seemed
to many of us more provincial Americans the exclusive property

* Reprinted from *The American Scholar*, Winter Issue, 1955–1956, pp.
69–79.

of the *Daily Worker*. People in India are no doubt still making trips to Benares in search of nirvana, but when their principal leaders speak they sound like members of Henry Wallace's dimly remembered Progressive party. Or, to cite another illustration, in Brazil's São Paulo, one skyscraper is going up beside another almost as fast as sodas line up on a counter; and when I was recently there admiring their assorted sizes and symmetries, there was a guest performance of the Folies Bergères in the dingy old opera house, and the true centers of culture were incredibly baroque movie theaters, the marble steps of which one climbed in state to see Marilyn Monroe.

Two things may, perhaps, be said in general about these trends. First, there is present in them a desire for a new way of looking from the inside of man at the outside world, and like all novel and, indeed, revolutionary decisions, this desire has lately very profoundly affected education. Second, the world feels, whether it approves or is hostile, that this way is what the masters of human society at present live by and inculcate, these masters being the United States and Russia. Obviously it is not easy to explain what the "new way" is, and one's endeavor to do so will depend pretty much on the situation in which one happens to find oneself. The world is full of places where nothing could be worse than it has been in terms of human welfare. These are areas in which primitive cultures have stood still, or in which once great and luxuriant civilizations have petered out. A farmer who ploughs worn-out soil with a forked stick and is then unable to shoo the rabbits from his spindly cereal crop because rabbits are sacred and must therefore be treated with the utmost courtesy is in a serious plight, indeed. Since there are unfortunately many who resemble him, it makes sense to reform his attitudes and methods, difficult though it may be.

Nevertheless, such reforms must be paid for. There are important differences between a life spent in the contemplation of the whole of being, and one which is devoted to the employment of that part of being which is immediately useful. It may seem only sheer common sense to settle for that which provides prosperity and comfort, but, alas, man is a creature who cannot be satisfied that way. He seems forever to be shortchanging either his body or his soul, and unless he can deal honestly with both, happiness is for him impossible. He can have everything tangible and still be profoundly miserable; he can possess nothing anyone could lay his hands on and still be quite jubilant. Hence the mysterious misery of our race. Were it not for this disease, bred into the marrow of our bones, we should have no literature, art, or religion. And we cannot do without them.

And so our world is also full of places where only the queer and the benighted still till the ground with broomsticks, but where, possibly because they cannot make up their minds to choose between the "whole" and the "part," people entertain no great longing for the "new way." These are primarily the areas in which the civilization of the Old World, nurtured by Greece and Rome and revitalized by Christianity, is either indigenous or has come into being through one form or other of cultural penetration. Here one almost invariably finds a group—a majority or a minority—which desires no radical change, and another group which is strongly in favor of it for various reasons. The debate between these is argued on various levels, but more frequently than not there ensues a shift of ground on both sides, depending largely on what the influence of the centers of world power, Washington and Moscow, is at a given moment. This influence may be very brazen or very subtle. It will be resented and opposed, welcomed and applauded, but it will be absorbed into the blood stream of the national mind.

Thus it seems that throughout Europe younger intellectuals have veered away from the philosophic disciplines toward education in technical subjects and in the sciences underlying them. René d'Harcourt reported that this was the case in France as early as 1948, and it would seem that the trend has been even more pronounced since that time. In Germany, a public opinion poll (American influence this, for better or worse) conducted by younger social scientists to determine the "prestige value" of the several professions, indicated, though the sampling may have been too limited, that insofar as the general population is concerned the professor still enjoys the greatest social respect. Yet the reason, the analysts say, is that in Germany the ultimate authority to which one turns when local medicos run out of hope is the teacher of medicine in a university clinic. For the younger generation, the engineer or the master of business administration stands, however, second on the list. It is of some lugubrious interest to note that professional writers fare very poorly in the poll. This for a country presumably reared in the shadow of Schiller and Goethe is strange news indeed. But the fact remains that both religion and philosophy are, intellectually speaking, much more vigorous in Germany than in the United States, particularly among members of the scientific professions.

Since West Germany is probably the part of the world in which the example of the United States is most zealously followed, it may be well to consider at this point, as realistically as conditions permit, what people outside think that example is. I believe one may approach the phenomenon from three sides. First, there is the formula for getting things done. That is, finding some *thing* to do the work for some *one*. Let me, at the risk of boredom, make the point in autobiographical terms. My grandfather was lured to Wisconsin from his home in Pennsylvania by the blandishments of one who must have been for those days a clever real-estate salesman. When he arrived to survey his manorial estate, into which he had put all his savings, he found ten acres of cleared land on the edge of which was a log house and a barn, a hundred and sixty acres of virgin forest, and an orchard. For years he supported the family by peddling the orchard fruit, meanwhile working as hard as he could to clear more land. But when, after the close of the First World War, his farm was sold, the first thing the new owner did was to cut down the orchard. The reason was, of course, simple. One cannot work an orchard with a tractor and a reaper. This straightforward deed has always seemed to me a symbol of the logic by which my time has lived. There is a great deal to be said for it, and naturally it is being said in many parts of the world.

The second visible side of the American phenomenon is in a way more beguiling. Just as the machine has freed man's arms, so it has also liberated his feet. Not even the most opulent of our cities possesses sufficient attractions to keep people in them when escape is possible. On week ends they travel bumper to bumper to houses with trees around them so that, apparently, the family fathers can stand in cellars, behind knotty-pine bars, ladling out the products of the distilling industry. And when the spirit is really weary, a simple remedy is at hand. One can take a plane to Paris, sip the beverages of Montmartre, and improve the soul by diving into Notre Dame and the Louvre. To be sure, all this costs money, which the income-tax collector is always infernally trying to take away; but as the travel statistics indicate, he is either far less crafty or more indulgent than his reputation would seem to suggest. At any rate, the ability of the American to carpet the European landscape (and some others as well) with a beguiling hue of green is one of the aspects of his life at which culturally undeveloped aliens both marvel and shake their heads. To think of a country in which the schoolteachers, despite their reputations for abject poverty, can take off in droves for guided tours through almost everywhere anyone can suggest is enough to give the local spectator a sense of dizziness in altitudes to which he can never aspire.

The third side is unfortunate. It is vacuity. Just why so many educated, and indeed often semiliterate, foreigners believe that the average American devotee to the free enterprise system is a nit-wit with no interest in higher values cannot easily be discovered. While Douglas Bush, most acidulous of Harvard professors, in diagnosing the contemporary culture of his country, reports that there are more earnest students of letters than he has ever pre-viously encountered, and while candidates for the contemplative Trappist Order have reached an unprecedented total in this country, judgment of the outside world on American culture has attained to a hitherto inaccessible nadir. I surmise that one of the principal explanations can be found in the fact that the char-acter of what Germans were wont to call the *Herrschaften* from

America has changed. These are no longer gentlemen from Yale and Princeton interested in conferring about intellectual problems, but citizens concerned with the baser things of life.

Yet there is something else which needs documentation, though none exists now, and it is beyond my ability to supply it. Casserley and Sorokin have both emphasized, though their methods of doing so are diverse, that a "culture of the senses" is the corollary of "romantic love." And one surmises that the frank, often almost barbaric way in which these find expression among us, appears to the rest of the world naïve and shocking, however rotten at the core it may itself be. The climate of the United States would seem to be doing to the Caucasoid man much the same as it did to his presumably Mongoloid precursor. It is making him tall, lean, bronzed, and naked. Unquestionably a certain readiness to resort to tomahawks and war whoops goes along with this development. When I was stationed in Bavaria, I happened to come to the little city of Niala, perched very close to the Iron Curtain separating West Germany from East. It was an industrial community which depended for much of its livelihood upon a sizable shoe factory. The population had been swelled by more than a thousand deportees who were either quartered on the citizenry or housed in a camp, this decidedly down at the heels. Nevertheless, in three years the town had not known a single case of homicide. This, in the light of American experience, was a remarkable fact.

I concluded that killing somebody, which is a messy business even when one is not caught doing it, presupposes a reasonably engrossing motive. There was probably little reason for slaughtering others for their money in Niala. Of course, people are known who slay their fellow men for the fun of it, but either none of this sort was in town or the tools for the job were lacking. But there is something else. Romantic love is obviously a major source of homicidal impulses, and it is probable that not a single case of this variety of love could be found in all Niala. There, if a working girl is not very refined, she gets herself in a family way and is then, as a matter of course, married off to the boy. If she is more sedate, she puts an ad in the paper listing her assets and her charms, and selects from the respondents the man deemed most likely to appreciate her and her worldly possessions. Finally, if she be truly idealistic in this Catholic community, she will behave as much like the Virgin Mary as possible and secure a husband who appreciates that kind of girl.

But a civilization like ours is made to order for romantic love. It is not merely that being interested in your prospective bride's accumulation of living room furniture and goose-feather-filled pillows would seem to us fearfully mercenary—which it perhaps is. The major fact is that her beauty, grace, and sparkling wit will presumably occupy pleasantly the hours not spent in finding the money with which to support her. This is one of the ways in which what was the luxury of a civilization dominated by idle aristocrats has permeated the whole culture of a society that has distributed leisure. Professor Casserley has argued lucidly and persuasively that the principal modern problem is how to extend to working masses liberated from drudgery by technological advances, the cultural advantages which, subsequent to the great revolutions of the past, were shared by the middle classes. He is quite right, and if one defines "cultural advantages" as he does, the goal is eminently desirable. Well, we have now lighted the fire of romantic love in nearly every heart, with the help of all known mass media of communication. And we realize, I trust, that for the presence or absence of it men and women alike can kill, with uncanny precision and reckless abandon. Alas, one must add that for millions this kind of love turns out to be one hundred per cent hokum. In a short while bulges appear on Sylvia's hips and knots on her legs. Her wit is merely a "line" which once recited has no sequel; and the only way to talk to her is to turn on television. Small wonder, perhaps, that the rest of the world, looking at and listening to the endless variations of romantic love which we peddle abroad with uninhibited abandon, should ask whether civilization is wholly safe in our hands.

On the other hand there is Russia, which advertises its product as the "new way" in its simon-pure state. In some respects its

Communist ruling class can advance relatively legitimate claims to glory. It has, at great cost to the freedom and welfare of individuals, promoted the development of industry and with that the production of usable merchandise. Whether the price paid was higher, in terms of human suffering, than that exacted when capitalism was foisted on western Europe is a moot question. I am inclined to think it cannot have been more than four or five times greater. The major difference is that, certainly in the cases of British and German capitalist exploitation, less than half a century passed before compelling voices were calling for the cessation of its abuses. The beginning of the end of industrial serfdom in both countries dates back at least a hundred years, and the major reason was freedom of the press, of religion, and of assembly. No such liberties have been granted to the Russian people since 1917, and of course they enjoyed them only sporadically prior to that time.

Recently a number of writers have contended that the key to the enigma of Russia is that its people are by nature anarchical, and have argued that therefore their government must of necessity exercise constraining force. Perhaps they have found some sort of solution of the riddle. Authorities on Russian religion, Berdyaev and Von Eckardt among them, have long since stressed the antipathy to organization and authoritative teaching which they deem to have been characteristic of the orthodox faith in its noblest days. And when one reads accounts of the Revolution by Feodor Stepun and others, a vision arises of peasants who for no plausible reason, save possibly a dream of benefits somehow likely to accrue to them, made government by suppression possible for Lenin. It seems to me, at any rate, that this interpretation makes much more sense than does any other of which I know.

Perhaps the strength of the Russian version of the "new way" has been derived from the two sources thus briefly indicated. On the one hand, there is abroad a feeling, difficult to dispel, that although up to this time the Communist revolution has been a disillusioning experience, the day will soon dawn when its success will be shown to be complete and overwhelming. And on the other hand, it is half unconsciously surmised that the followers of Lenin have fully reckoned with what is anarchical—which means, opposed to discipline and social constraint—in human nature, and will therefore establish a social order more palatable than what has seemingly become the norm in the United States.

In my opinion, we have gravely underestimated the appeal which regimentation has for untold millions of human beings. Even the Protestant religions in the United States are strongest when, as do the Lutherans and the Methodists, they prescribe a stern code for their adherents. The notion that each person should be free to act within the light of his own conscience may well be truly possible only for those who have very recently been emancipated from the bonds of dogma. To us generally it may seem that allegiance to the Hegelian-Marxist-Leninist doctrine is both irrational and constrictive; and no doubt nations like the Hungarians and the Poles, who have lived under its prophets, will agree. Yet large numbers of other men do not. To them the United States looks like a factory in which all the spindles turn while the people who operate them are all a bit tipsy. In Russia being tipsy is presumably not allowed.

All this helps to account for the partial success of the Communist peace propaganda. Superficially considered, nothing seems more absurd than that the Russians, who have violated countless agreements and started conflicts wherever they deemed them desirable, should be feeding the dove of peace in their cote. But if we bear in mind what manner of folk the world thinks we are, the riddle is easier to solve. The Kremlin can keep the peace if it so desires. But if some United States Senator or general decides that war is a good idea and drums up enough support, what insurance has the rest of the world against Armageddon? This queer notion is, I believe, slowly dying out, but it has been for a long time the most formidable weapon in the Soviet propaganda arsenal.

But there is no doubt that it is the Russian use of education which most markedly defines communism in action at the present time. In order to secure control of the schools in Hungary, for instance, the Kremlin and its stooges fought an epic battle with the Catholic Church. What has emerged is a system one can perhaps best describe as Jesuit teaching of the humanistic period stood upon its head. The idea which underlay that teaching was to make available to pupils the great literature of classical antiquity and then to fuse this with Catholic doctrine and motivation. Communism in Hungary (and of course elsewhere) sets out with the determination to make education serve as the instrument for disseminating technological skills, because only these prepare for the kind of life which will help transform society into the *summum bonum*—a smoothly functioning unit of production. On this, courses in the ideology of communism are superimposed. These run all the way from a kind of secularized Sunday school for the workers, to highly specialized indoctrination at the university level. What one can learn about its textbooks and methods is of great interest because manifestly little time is spent in dissecting Marx and Lenin, and very much on proving that the Communist state is an ideal incarnation of what America is popularly supposed to be—a place which exists in order to make wheels turn efficiently and so raise the standard of living. And of course queer things happen. After having got its educational system going full blast in Hungary, meanwhile gouging the peasants and herding them into collective farming, it was discovered that one of Europe's breadbaskets was without food and that there was no place to put the quickly trained young devotees of technology! One of the minor grim notes in Prime Minister Rákosi's many addresses explaining why things had gone to pot was a reference to young ladies trained in typing and stenography. These he said would be given jobs by the government doing manual labor. And as a result of all this there unquestionably exists behind the Iron Curtain a vast anticlerical movement —in the sense of opposition to the reigning clerical caste—which corrodes ideological orthodoxy even though it is wholly impotent to influence in any way the use of the vast technological machine which the government has created and controls.

I now come belatedly to the moral about education which

seemingly needs to be appended. The Russian problem is how to keep the machines going in their industrial paradise. In this basket are all their eggs that can still be hatched. Our wheels do turn, thank God, and of course we must see to it that they continue to do so. The major problem for us is the conquest of vacuity through education, because vacuity is the result of the leisure which technology makes possible. For the first time in history great masses of people find themselves surrounded by vast reaches of space and time; and if you do not know what to do with space, it defines itself as emptiness, and time moves into a sort of twilight shared with eternity. Leisure, surmised Georges Bernanos cynically, is that from which one escapes by going to work. And of course the reason why men can be so driven is the dreadful nakedness of the self in isolation when one has not encountered it previously. To find one's soul when one has not dreamed it existed may well be for many, especially those belonging to a culture which has expressed itself so energetically in action, a quite unnerving shock.

And so the schoolboy who now turns his shining face to the future must no longer be trained merely for the tasks he is to perform. He will need the twin modes of intellectual life which are interior discipline and outgoing dialogue, because only so can he exist with a measure of happiness during the long hours when some *thing* does his work for *him*. It is not necessary for me to say where such an education can find the precepts and the methods it requires. They are the legacy of the aristocratic past, which must now become the democratic future. All this, of which the Russian is not officially permitted to think, has now become that which we must have in our minds if we are to endure.

HISTORICISM
AND LITERATURE*

PROFESSOR GRIERSON HAS NOTED THAT EVERY CREATIVE PERIOD IN literature is imperiled by "feelings" seeking to override the judgment. And I suppose, since it would hardly be fitting that a student of general literature should do more than surmise, that the pattern of historical study designed by the historicist is suggested primarily by feeling. The term historicism is of course used somewhat narrowly here. It is taken to stand for the acceptance of history as evidence from which the psychologist can deduce the ebb and flow of man's ethical and aesthetic idealism. The practitioner must feel his way toward the pulse of change. Dilthey coined for him the agreeable term *Einfuehlung*. It is clear that the great critics and historians of antiquity held a different view of their crafts. They thought that resolute and meticulous study of the facts could lay bare the logic of progression from point to point in the story of human decisions, passions, wisdom, and weakness. But the historicist speaks of "points" only as semicolons which mark the varying, sundering movements on the sea of collective cultural change.

Undoubtedly not all he has said or done is bad. By no means. At bottom he may well have been tormented by his sense of the superiority of creative artist to critic or scholar, and so have wished himself to hold the mirror up to his own mind, and therewith presumably to nature. If he could sit down with his subject, coddle him, and get out of him secrets he might not

* Reprinted from *The Journal of Bible and Religion* 14 (1946), pp. 135–138.

otherwise confide except under duress to his own conscious mind, the historian could suppose that he too had dwelt in the light of the creative imagination. And one may well note that when John Galsworthy wrote about the "Creation of Character in Literature" near the close of his career, he did so in words which might almost have been used by Dilthey. We may concede that the standard exercise of the critical faculty has a certain almost pharisaical woodenness. Against this Wordsworth, for example, protested. "One impulse from the vernal wood" does not indeed actually supplant Plato and Isaiah. But one has sometime to revert to the stance of mind and heart which Plato and Isaiah themselves adopted, and see things, experiences, rather than mere words about things, experiences.

An embarrassing problem arises only when he goes on to assume that the tide of experience can be tested by anything less than a norm. And historicism seems to me based on just such an assumption. To say that the record of an era can be understood only as the product of the impulses of that era is to take it for granted that there is really something like an era; that is, a period of time which actually has its beginning and end within itself. Naturally there are dramas within historical time, which can be said to have *dénouement* and *finale*. But these dramas are not eras, if only because man and dog are, after all, constants. The other day I happened to read a description by an eighteenth century German writer of his dachshund; and what he had written was an admirable portrait of the wholly indispensable little fiend who is in my household. Men also do certain things constantly and apart; and therefore they do not do them merely within a segment of time.

Here I may illustrate. If one asks why the "Prize Song" does not lend itself so well to choral singing as does "Jingle Bells," the answer is not that the one is lofty and the other inane. Sometimes I can't help thinking that the English round is a more distinguished lyric than Wagner's. It is rather a simple matter of rhythm, and consequently of physics, which decrees that a certain movement of sound is more easily memorized and synchronized than another. This is the sort of circumstance over which man has no control, any more than he can control the fact that when his military antagonist is well-equipped with antitank guns no tank attack can succeed. On the other hand, there are aspects of human experience, or rather, there are solid, substantial verities in human experience, which are goverened by a totally different kind of law. Recently I returned from Europe on a transport inhabited by some sixty-five hundred soldiers. There were four servings of each mess. Then after two days the loud-speaker announced that tickets would be issued to all the men, and woe betide anybody who showed up in the wrong line. What had happened was that some particularly hungry GI's, fed at six, were famished again at half-past eight and enticed to go back for another meal. Here is the sort of action over which man has control. There is no law of psysics which compels a man to stalk the prey of food in this manner. The fact that a rule exists which is of his own making is the supreme constant of man's history.

Literature is story or symbol, and these are concerned always with both types of conduct referred to. On the one hand, the art of writing affords a record and interpretation of man's experience with nature, that is, abstractly, with physical and chemical necessity or alternatives. The rain falls on the just and the unjust alike. The gods have their sport with Tess. If a man chooses to bring up his family on a Vermont hillside, the air they breathe will be different from that inhaled by children reared in Brooklyn. On the other hand, literature mirrors man's decisions. It deals with that which is unpredictable in him because he himself is the source of the prediction. Why should Lear have "evolved" to the point of deciding that his daughters were to be put to a love test, or why should Othello have been such an idiot about a handkerchief? Of course, Lear may have been "predisposed" to such actions, and Othello's past may help explain why he was unaware of the annoying habit even beautiful and virtuous women have of dropping things. But they didn't have to act as they did. It is quite clear that both were dreadful fools, guilty of pride and jealousy. Shakespeare may not have been very lucid about a number of things. He is very clear about this.

No good writer ever constructed a convincing character on any other basis. Even Joyce's young man, beset with millions of not very edifying thoughts, is nevertheless a person who could have thought of something else if he had wished to do so. But let me digress for the sake of a quite different example. Robert Bridges writes: "When it was ordered in 1549 that the English Psalms should be sung in Church instead of the Latin, there was no music to which they could be sung save the Latin church-tunes. These two things, the English words and the Latin music, were incompatible. This had not been suspected." Somebody gave the order, in short, without thinking matters through. But the laws of sound being what they are, something had to be done. Either the order had to be changed, or the music had to be re-written.

The trouble with historicism is, first, that it is interested in everything about an order or a decision except the ordering and the deciding. It can offer a very piquant account of how and why people were gradually brought to the point where singing hymns in English seemed preferable to singing them in Latin, but the fiat to do so disappears from view. And, second, the trouble is that the limiting natural circumstance which hems in human action does not have, for the historicist, any design. But great literature cannot ever, does not ever, assume that the natural world is without design. "Euclid alone has looked on beauty bare," says Miss Millay. And all the past and present of poetry declares Amen.

About these two observations I should like to say another earnest word. That there is design in nature, pattern, sequence, purpose, surely nobody will any longer deny. For now we know that when the smallest thing in the world, namely the atom, is not kept where it belongs, even the biggest things will disintegrate. It may be true, as Kant argued, that the design does not necessarily prove the existence of a creative Designer. But one may certainly say that the absence of design would prove nothing, because we should not be around to make the demonstration. Man may crave a different, more comfortable design than the one which exists. But he has, in every fundamental sense, to accept what he is given as it is. And in like manner I believe that by analogy, at least, we must assume that some kind of design must apply to human conduct. To concede that the individual may do anything he likes is to grant him the right to make much more than a confounded nuisance of himself. Plato and Aristotle, followed by Christian tradition in this, tried to deduce the design of human conduct from the nature of man even as cosmic design is deducible from cosmic nature. It has been the custom of late to sweep this philosophy aside and to look for such design as there may be in the necessity for socializing the basic pleasure-pain impulses. This attempt has left us all seriously befuddled, tragically so, I think, but at least there is implicit in it the admission that some kind of conduct design simply has to be projected.

Now I believe that great literature has been in perennial quest of design in the sense indicated. This quest is pointed in three directions. First, there is formal design. The patterns of prose and verse are not arbitrary or fortuitous. Whether they be organic, that is, suited orchestrally to the movement of impressions or ideas, or static, they are creations, sometimes the very bosom children of genius. They undoubtedly evolve, but not blindly. When one has seen, for instance, what Petrarch and Milton made of the "little song," the *sonnetto,* one is grateful to the artist who first framed the measure, but even more deeply indebted to the great masters who perfected it. Observing the slow ripening of form to perfection, for example, the maturing of blank verse, is fascinating, as Brunetière observed. But there is nothing casual or blind about that development. It is derived from patient personal insight into the laws of art structure.

Second, there is visualization of the relationship, the harmony or dissonance, between man and his environment. Wordsworth was happy in the hills; Sinclair Lewis was unhappy in Gopher Prairie. It is the function of literature to adjust man to his neigh-

borhood, to make the universe habitable for him. There are tides
of fashion about environment. Pope was blissful in a Twickenham
which would have made Keats squirm. To find out why is a
pleasant historical enterprise. But environment is not all fashion.
Nobody has yet longed for constant drought or incessant rain.
It is unrecorded that anybody has welcomed a crash of light-
ning into his living room. And I suppose that not even hermits
are wholly indifferent to the moon, which indeed merits a kind
of gloss. No London poet has written much about it, presumably
because he so seldom has had the opportunity to see it. And
practically every German poet has, because German poets are
normally country folk.

Finally, there is design in human conduct. We are such stuff
as dreams are made of. But not quite. We write letters on a page
which has been lettered a thousand times before. Our most spectacular originality is only palimpsest. Yet, unless the letters spell
out certain words, the result is agony. It is no good trying to
derive the basic norms of conduct from the climate, the stars, or
folk taboos. If you kill, the man is dead and blood is on your
hands. If you covet your neighbor's goods, you immerse yourself
in the consuming passion for goods. Some peoples may have held
life or goods in lesser esteem than we. It has latterly grown
doubtful. But no folk has ever held life or goods in absolute dis-
esteem.

In short, great literature is not concerned with great thoughts
merely, but with great verities also. Historicism at best is concerned with great thoughts, but not with verities. There is little
else one need say.

But something further may, nevertheless, be said. There is
a certain modern literature which assumes, for instance, that
philandering is a normal human pastime. I sometimes fancy it
not the product of an era, but rather of a tragic childishness
which recurs in all immature eras. You might dole out four
women (or five) to every man, and vice versa, as you might serve
four helpings of fish. Only then the man, or the woman, would
be like fish. That may be quite all right. But you can't have it

both ways. Fish write very dull books. And, on the other hand, there is a kind of criticism which seems to believe that one must write only nice things about people, because otherwise somebody might acquire improper ideas. After two thousand years of Christendom, it should be sufficiently evident that the world is in need of redemption because it is the kind of world it is. Perhaps both these varieties of specious writing buttress the historicist contention. For both are products of taboos.

In conclusion, let me repeat that the historicist school is not without merit. It discovered methodologically the complexity out of which the work of art derives its complex character. The concept of evolution it sponsored led to the valuable discovery of growth. If now I append a few words about the Bible, I am sure that it will be evident that I do not speak as a theologian, which unfortunately I am not, but as a literary historian of sorts.

The great new value which has presented itself to Scripture study is a sense of progression, of the actual course of living. Our fathers read the Good Book as a sequence of maxims, and profited notably thereby when they were careful to make due allowance for the complementary, sometimes contrasted, sayings which the Bible uses to explore the whole of human existence. But they did not often, perhaps they did not ever, possess insight into several very important and absorbing traits of the narrative. First, they could not sense as do we the continuing pertinence of the social ethic which the prophetic tradition enshrines, and so they could not really understand how the New Testament grew out of the Old. Second, they were without the historical lore needed to comprehend in a measure the tremendous significance of the nearness of the towering personality of the Master to the infant Church which wrote and talked about Him. In particular, the character of print as a literary vehicle restrained them from recreating for themselves the virility of the older oral tradition upon which all civilization then relied. They could not know what the Torah had once been, and so what the Christian urge to supply a Christian Torah implied. Finally, they did not grasp, as we can now that the critics have spoken, the fact that inspiration has a necessary relationship to all forms of in-spiriting; and so they were always in danger of limiting the Sacred Spirit to a mechanical dictation process.

These are, as every educator knows, some of the new insights which are now transforming the Bible into a very real and a very contemporary book. But it would be very much too bad if our delight in these good things led us ever to forget that the Bible is not only a book which became a book, but also a book which has something to say; that, in short, it is meaningless as literature if it is meaningless as revelation. We must see to it that the old temptation to find literary and aesthetic pleasure does not rob us of the ancient hard lesson rooted in the constant sacrifice of which the Scripture speaks. Of course there is always a danger lest all literature be suffered to become mere pleasant-ness. But certainly the Bible cannot ever be that if the enraptured souls who transcribed its message are not to be betrayed.